GRACED

Ray Bevan

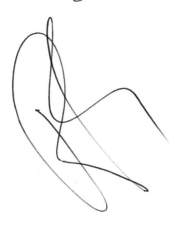

A PRACTICAL GUIDE
TO GRACE BASED LIVING

Edited by Joanne O'Sullivan.

Published for Ray Bevan by Verité CM Limited,
124 Sea Place, Worthing, West Sussex BN12 4BG
+44 (0) 1903 241975

email: enquiries@veritecm.com
www.veritecm.com

British Library Cataloguing in Publication Data

A catalogue record for this book is available from
the British Library

ISBN: 978-1-914388-35-4

Design and Print Management by Verité CM Ltd
www.veritecm.com

COMMENDATIONS

I have been blessed by Pastor Ray Bevan and his ministry is one that exalts Christ and His finished work. This book 'Graced' will inspire you and give you a fresh revelation of God's amazing grace. Read this book and receive a fresh touch from God!

Pastor Lawrence Lim, *New Creation Church, Singapore*

As a young man I sat in Sunday School and heard the amazing stories on how mighty people in the Bible did tremendous things. In Hollywood, where I live, there is a term, 'the back story' that means what really happened. Ray Bevan is one of the best at bringing the Bible to life. I've watched him on the largest conference platforms in the world. He has mastered the art of explaining and exploring stories that bring change from the Bible. In his new book, he shows how God used unstable people to do sturdy projects. He takes us chapter by chapter on how Grace prevails in all situations and circumstances. This book will build your faith and cause you to move forward with a fresh outlook and a new supernatural strength.

Tim Storey, *Author, Speaker, Life Coach*

After working for Ray for more than thirteen years as his Personal Assistant, I can honestly say that Ray lives what he preaches, both on and off the platform. I have had the privilege to watch up-close as his grace-filled words have revived many Churches and Church leaders worldwide, encouraging and inspiring others to finish strong.

I have marvelled as Ray has continued to minister through the ups and downs of everyday life, always trusting and always believing for the best – looking first and foremost to the Word of God and His Spirit for guidance.

Ray is wise counsel, authentic, and a father in the faith – please listen to what Ray has to say – he is the real deal!

Hayley Corley

Ray Bevan is a dear friend and he has a real revelation of God's grace. I've heard him preach it; I've seen him live it. He has blessed me so many times as he unpacks God's stance towards humanity. I am sure this book is going to help and bless a lot of people.

Andreas Nielsen, *Lead Pastor, Hillsong Church, Sweden*

I love the profound sense of freedom and joy with which Ray Bevan ministers the grace of God. He is a prophetic voice to the Church today and teaches with an anointing and depth of wisdom that is able to have a significant impact on the Church. Having been impacted by Ray's preaching and teaching for twenty years, it has been a privilege to come to know him as a friend over the last ten years and witness the way his faith through life's challenges has produced a longevity of ministry that is inspiring.

Richard van der Kolk, *Lead Pastor, Hillsong Church, The Netherlands and Brussels*

I have known Ray since 1980 when we both had hair! We toured together arounf the UK and Spain with a Christian band called 'Frontline', he became a good friend and was the 'best man' at my wedding (a debatable title, I have to say!) Ray excelled as a lead vocalist, but also as a Preacher/ Evangelist. His God-given gift meant he saw many hundreds of life-changing decisions being made, whether he preached the gospel from a circus tent, from a church platform, sat around a table or chatting in a bus queue. For decades he has faithfully served the church to the best of his ability and anointing. Ray was, and is, a gift on legs!

The Gospel he himself embraced clearly shaped his life and so did the revelation of grace that God gave him years on. Ray's life has not been without adversity, but that understanding of grace has enabled him to flourish in the toughest of times.

I'm grateful we all get to taste the truth of God's grace in this book. It is written by someone who doesn't write about grace as subject matter, but as one who has experienced its power time after time through life. Read it with an open heart

Steve Dixon, *Hillsong Church, Brisbane, Australia*

For many of us, grace seems tricky to define – and even more challenging to accept. My friend Ray Bevan is passionate about grace. His understanding of grace has been forged on lofty hilltops and in some dark valleys. Over a lifetime of ministry, it has given him a special connection with people who live in dark corners beyond the church. It has also compelled him to share with Christians around the world what it means to be truly free. In this book, he shares not just his teaching on grace, but his experience of it. I pray that it inspires you to live in the fulness of God's grace and truth.

Mal Fletcher, *Founder 2030Plus*

Ray Bevan is one of the most insightful men of the scriptures that I know. His ability and anointing to share the depth of scripture is amazing. 'Graced' will bless you beyond description!

Pastor John Jenkins, *First Baptist Church, Glenarden, USA*

I have known Ray and his ministry for many years, and he is a great friend of mine, my wife Zelda and family. He has great insight into the subject of grace. It's a 'gamechanger' and will impact your life.

Pastor Ray Macauley, *Founding Pastor, Rhema Church, South Africa*

ACKNOWLEDGEMENTS

I would like to thank the congregation of the King's Church, Newport, those that sat under my ministry from 1989 to 2016. Thank you for your hunger to receive the Word of grace. A hunger which caused me to prioritise my time as your Pastor to seek fresh manna every week for over twenty-five years, much of the content of this book is the result.

I would like to thank my family and friends for encouraging me to keep true to my calling in the face of self-doubt and personal heartbreak; particularly my stepdaughter Marit and my granddaughter Eva.

Thank you to Hayley and Noel Corley; Anne Matthews; Pastor David and Emma Morgan; Bobby and Yvonne Ball; Terry and Barbara Law and many more who, if mentioned, would be a book in itself.

Thank you to all those who walked away when I needed your support, you taught me how to trust grace alone and thus delivered me from approval addiction.

Thanks to Joanne O'Sullivan who spent hours editing this book, amplifying my words so that they can be clearly understood.

And of course, thank You, Holy Spirit as You reached into the treasures of Heaven's vaults, particularly concerning the grace-soaked truth of the finished work of Christ and it's riches of the New Covenant – divine spices that marinated my heart and left me breathless as I experienced the gasp of Grace.

CONTENTS

INTRODUCTION

'Unless you become like a little child you cannot see (understand) the Kingdom of God'.

The incredible significance of those words never really impacted me until I began to discover revelationally and experientially the amazing world of Grace alone. The grace of God goes beyond the realm of intellect and theological explanation, and in my view can only be truly appreciated when we embrace it through the perspective of a child. Let me try to explain what I mean.

My Granddaughter, in one conversation, taught me more about how we should experience the grace of God than all the books I had ever read on the subject. We were sitting in my garden talking about her world, when out of the blue she asked me a question that was used by the Holy Spirit to lead me into a wonderful truth.

"How old are you *Bampa*?" she asked with wide inquisitive eyes.

'I am sixty-five', I answered. I waited for a verbal response but was met with her innocent searching eyes brimming with tears. Concerned about her sudden intensity of emotion I tried to comfort her and asked why she was crying.

"I don't want you to die, *Bampa!*" she replied. Trying to console her, I told her I wasn't going to die for many years but at the same time hoping deep down I was prophesying that truth to my own heart.

"But you will be one hundred soon," she replied, "and everyone dies when they are a hundred". Not knowing what to say I noticed that suddenly her facial expression changed from to despair and grief to one of hope and wonder, you know that look of wonder that was depicted on the face of Elliot when he saw ET for the first time? She wiped her tears and said, "I know what to do *Bampa*, I am going to make you thirty!" She was convinced that what she was about to do was the answer to alleviate her fear of losing her *Bampa*. That look of absolute conviction emanated from her beautiful little face was so honest and pure I started to believe that whatever she was about to tell me would happen.

"How are you going to do that Eva?" I asked. She looked at me as if I couldn't calculate a simple mathematical equation like one plus one.

"Fairy dust" she replied, her chin in the air, as if I was the only one on the planet that didn't know.

"Where are you going to get fairy dust from?" I asked. She was now getting really impatient with my ignorance and boldly declared,

"Tinkerbell of course! She sent the tooth fairy to my room last night and left me one-pound coin and a bag of fairy dust, I'm going to throw it over you, and you will become thirty!".

In the middle of this very magical conversation with my Granddaughter the word of Jesus kept reminding me of the truth, '*unless you become as a little child you will never see or understand the secrets and blessings of my Kingdom*'. Realizing the Holy Spirit was about to teach me a vitally important lesson and not wanting to shatter the fairy tale expectation of my Granddaughter, I went along with the whole plan.

"Are you ready *Bampa*?"

"I am" I said, and rolled up my sleeves, "Let's do this". As she threw the fairy dust over me (I'm still trying to get it off my clothes) I pretended something was happening to my body, "What's happing Eva? My whole body is tingling!". With absolute conviction of success, she replied,

"Don't fight it *Bampa*, its magic!" Finally, when I stopped shaking, I said,

"What just happened?"

"Bampa" she replied, "You are now thirty" and walked away to play with her dolls. Her heart at total peace believing the fairy dust had done its work. As she walked away, I felt the Holy Spirit say to me again *unless you become like a little child, unless you believe what I can do in your life as much as your Granddaughter believes the fairy dust has made you thirty, you will never appreciate the wonder of my Grace*. I began to realize in my study of the doctrine of Grace I had missed its whole essence. If I could explain theologically or intellectually the essence of Grace, I would never understand it at all. Unless we enter the world of wonder; the unexplainable; the indescribable. The Grace of God would remain just another topic to preach in a six-week series of Bible Studies.

Eva lives in the world of wonder, as do most children. She lives in a world where magic mirrors speak, where pumpkins become golden carriages and where wooden puppets become real boys. I started to think about the world God had brought me into through the new birth. A world that exists in another dimension. A world of unlimited opportunity, unexpected help, and unconditional love. A world where we can experience '*far above all we can ask or think*', the world of Grace alone. The desire in my heart as you read on is not to expand your theological understanding of Grace but for you to experience the wonder of it. As a result of that conversation with my Granddaughter my approach to the study of the Grace of God introduced me to a new realm. The realm of wonder.

For me 'a wonder' is when God does far above all we can ask or imagine. Psalm 77, verse 14 declares, '*You are the God who does wonders.* Moses never imagined that God would open the Red Sea and make a way where there was no way, but God did far above all he could imagine. That's the wonder of Grace. Joshua never imagined God would stop the rotation of the earth allowing him more time to complete his assignment, but God did far above all he could imagine. That's the wonder of Grace. The Disciples never imagined Jesus would speed up a thirty-year process of wine making to alleviate the embarrassment of a newlywed couple, but He did far above all they could imagine. That's the wonder of Grace, and what about the raising of Lazarus from the dead? Mary and Martha imagined Jesus healing their brother from sickness, but they never imagined Jesus raising him from the dead. That's the wonder of Grace. My prayer for you, is that you ask God to restore to you the wonder of Grace, to cultivate within you a childlike heart of wonder that supersedes logic, eradicates limited thinking and opens up to you a world that sounds like fairy tale but is in fact a glorious reality. The wonder of Grace is that it transports you to a world where nothing is impossible.

The Biblical incidents mentioned above, in all cases, things went from difficult to impossible. Very often we can imagine Jesus turning up when things are difficult. Mary and Martha could imagine Jesus turning up when it was difficult, but Jesus didn't just want to show them a healing he wanted to show them a wonder, where the unimaginable becomes a reality. What is it in your life right now that has gone from difficult to impossible? You've prayed, confessed, used up all the faith mechanics and still things have not improved. In fact, they've gone from difficult to impossible. All hope is gone, all your faith used up. It's time to start trusting God for a wonder, the wonder of Grace where God does for you far above all you can ask or imagine. His Grace works best when we give up trying to work it out. His Grace kicks in when we want to give up. What Red Sea are you faced with? What area of your life do you want time to stop or speed up? What or who lies behind a stone encased tomb dead and stinking with no hope of recovery? Trust God to show you a wonder. Unless you become like a little child the world of Grace cannot be accessed or experienced. It's time to enjoy the wonder of Grace.

CHAPTER ONE

AMBUSHED BY GRACE

You won't find the village *Resolven* as one of the top places of interest in the Welsh Tourist Board, or a place you 'Must visit' for historical significance. In fact, when people ask where I came from, I never say *Resolven*, not because I'm ashamed of the place of my birth, or place that I grew up, but because even Welsh people have a difficulty locating the little community. However, looking now from the vantage point of over sixty years of His-story in my life, I'm humbled to think that God not only knew where it was, but that is where He chose to place me on the planet to prepare and nurture me for what He had destined for me.

Never despise your beginnings however insignificant, turbulent or traumatic. God knows how to use it all as material that goes into the embroidery, the tapestry called your race, your purpose, your destiny.

The reason why I feel compelled to give you a brief overview of my life is because I believe the life-lessons I will share in this book carry more weight and authority when you know who I am. It worked negatively for Jesus when God thrust him into His calling at thirty years of age. The voices of Jesus' world shouted with cynicism *Who does He think He is?*

We know how he grew up; we know his siblings and, Nazareth? Of all places, has anything good come out of Nazareth? I'm praying that will not be the case as I share with you a potted history of my life but in fact, the opposite. I hope you will be encouraged to receive what I say as you discover who I am. I pray you will run your race with more hope and passion because you will receive encouragement for how Grace Alone has helped me to run mine.

HIS GRACE ALONE:

1. Gave me the repentance to turn to Him, Acts 11.10
2. His Grace gave me the faith to believe Him, 1 Corinthians 4:7; Acts 16:14
3. His Grace gave me the love to love Him, Romans 5:5
4. His Grace gave me the desire to serve him, Philippians 2:13
5. His Grace gave me the power to minister Him, Acts 1:4

6. His Grace gave me the authority to proclaim Him, 2 Corinthians 3:5-6; Romans 15: 15-16

7. His Grace gave me the fruit to manifest Him, Galatians 5

8. His Grace gave me the Godliness to be like Him, 2 Peter 1:3

9. His Grace gave me a place to be with him, John 14

10. His Grace gave me the righteousness to stand before Him, Romans 5:16-17

11. His Grace gave me the energy to work for Him, 1 Corinthians 15:10

12. His Grace gave me the gifts to help build His Church, 1 Peter 4:10; 1 Corinthians 12:11; Ephesians 4:16

13. His Grace gave me the security to endure, Philippians 1:6; Jude 24; 1 Corinthians 1:8

14. His Grace gave me the calling to change the world with His Gospel, 1 Corinthians 15:10

So, you can understand why I entitled this book, *Graced*

CHAPTER TWO

GRACE ALONE

My confidence concerning my future is the result of the realization of His Grace working in my past. Having a revelation of Grace Alone will deliver you not only from the guilt of the past but from the fear of the future. Why? Because Grace prepares a table for us to feast in the midst of famine. To dine in the presence of disaster and to eat without fear when surrounded by enemies. I once read a story about 'New College Oxford'. It's an amazing place and in 1990 a famous historian visited the college to delve into its historical past. As he was taken around the college by the tour guide, he asked how old the premises were. The tour guide replied, 'Well sir, it was built in 1386'. As he walked around the place with wonder, his eyes were drawn to the majestic oak beams that spanned the width of the building, holding up the heavy roof. 'Are those the original beams?' he asked.

'No' replied the guide, they were replaced in 1890.'

He went on to explain that the new beams, at that time, were around 100 years old and the reason how they were replaced is an amazing story in itself. In 1890 after around five-hundred years, the old beams needed replacing because the weight of the roof was too much for them. The problem was no one knew where to find beams long enough to span the width of the building. No one knew where to find giant oaks that size that were needed to replace the old beams. However, the college forester provided the answer. Hidden at the back of the college was a great stand of oaks. They were over five-hundred years old and were planted by the same man who fashioned and placed the original beams in 1386. Why? Because he knew ahead of time their strength would weaken and between four to five-hundred years later, they would need replacing. Knowing that, he had the foresight to plant replacements. Those five hundred years, the space between 1390 and 1890 were used to prepare the material for any future crisis. God has already prepared in advance everything you need for future crises. The joy you need when life has stolen your song. The love you need when someone has broken your heart. The peace you need when the storms of circumstance threaten your life.

Ephesians 2:10 'For we are His workmanship created in Christ for good works, *which God prepared beforehand that we should walk in them.'* (Emphasis added).

For every unbearable weight, every future trial, heartbreak, tragedy, disaster, storm and loss, God has already prepared what you need that will sustain you. He has even prepared for your unfaithfulness, rebellion and back sliding, look at the example of Jonah;

'Now the Lord had prepared a great fish to swallow Jonah' Jonah 1:17a (NKJV).

The same grace that carried you through past crisis, the same grace sustains you in your present crisis, is the same grace already prepared in advance for your future crisis.

The Welsh revival in the early 1900's was known as the singing revival, the Welsh love to sing, it runs through our culture like jam in a sponge pudding. My brother and I loved to sing. We fancied ourselves as the next *Everly Brothers* because, without sounding a little arrogant, we actually did sound a lot like them! In Wales, we have a national school singing competition called *Eisteddfod*. My brother and I developed our singing technique during our school days singing competitively and we did quite well. But our passion was to become pop stars, never realizing that in our early teens, schoolgirls would be writing our names on their satchels (school bags). Why? Because our dream became a reality when Decca Records signed us and released our first single in 1966 called 'This Little Bird'. The way it came about was the stuff of fairy tales.

My brother and I were singing the song in our bathroom. (Everyone sounds better singing in the bathroom because of the natural echo). I was 17 and my brother was 14. Unknown to us, our dulcet tones caught the attention of a recording buff who happened to be passing our house. He was so captivated with what he heard, he knocked the door and asked our mother who was producing the music? John Daniels took us over to his little recording studio (the outside toilet), and with a single guitar accompaniment we recorded *This Little Bird* and sent it to Decca records. We didn't have that much expectation of acceptance because a few years earlier, they had rejected a recording sent in by a local Liverpudlian band called The Beatles. You can imagine the rush we had when we were invited to London to sign a recording contract with Decca Records

The record was released, and our pop star status was born, well, in *Resolven* at least! We formed a band to start our professional career, although we had to wait until my brother was 15 (that's when you could finish school in those days). I quit my job as an apprentice painter and decorator and for the next five years was vacuumed into the 60's pop scene. Releasing more records and touring the clubs and dance halls of the UK. Even during that season, I believe, God had His hand on my life using all those experiences to prepare me for what lay ahead and protecting me by His grace from the 'anything goes' culture of the 'swinging 60's'.

As I look back, I remember feeling amidst all the excitement and irresponsibility of those days that I was born for something more. It all came to a head for me while sitting in the office of a music mogul named Mickey Most. He was the Simon Cowell of his day. Many artists would have given their right arm to be sitting where I was right then, but however exciting that opportunity was, it couldn't even come close to filling the growing emptiness that gaped within me. It was at that point I realized that showbiz was not for me. I left the band, settled down into a regular job and was engaged to my girlfriend believing that this was the way that would end my search for contentment. Within a few months, after realizing I could have made the biggest mistake of my life, I found myself in no man's land. I tried to reform the band and resurrect the dream of stardom but by then, the other members of the band had moved on including my brother who had embarked on a solo career leading him becoming a huge star in Canada with many hit records and TV appearances. So, here I was, feeling stuck, empty and lost until *The Greatest Story Ever Told*, came to our little village in *Resolven*. No, it wasn't a circus, it was the classic film depicting the life of Christ. Jesus came to *Resolven*. He knew where *I* was, He knew what I was searching for, and the time was right. The Holy Spirit made Jesus real to me in that cinema and my life was changed. I discovered Jesus was the end of my search and the beginning of the greatest adventure on the planet. The change was so radical my mother thought I was having a nervous breakdown. She could handle me drunk or stoned, but finding God? No one in our family had ever gone down that road. My fiancée was a Church goer, so I went to her Church, a small Pentecostal Church of about 70 people where we were married. I spent the next ten years there working out the early stages of my Salvation. The message of Grace Alone was alien to those sincere, law-bound believers then and the teaching I received didn't really help me overcome the many personal problems I was fighting with emotionally, mentally and spiritually. In fact, it took many years for the effects of legalism to evaporate from my life and even now, I find I must apply the Gospel of Grace to my heart and mind because of my bias towards performance based pharisee-ism.

The one thing those 10 years taught me, the one thing that little Church ingrained in me was a passion to reach people for Jesus. Looking back now, I realized my passion was a little fanatical and definitely unwise (singing and preaching on my front doorstep – reminding passers-by how sinful they were, did NOT help!). My passion for Church consumed my life. I was there Sunday morning, Sunday afternoon and Sunday night plus the early morning Saturday prayer meeting, the Tuesday night prayer meeting and the Thursday night Bible Study. On hindsight, (oh, the blessing of hindsight!) I now realize it was not the best way to lay a foundation in your marriage, especially when your wife does not share the same passion.

I threw myself into the life of the Church serving, working with children, basically doing anything I was asked. And even though, those early years were riddled with legalism, some of the great lessons that were marinated into my life were those of servanthood and commitment.

While my passion for Jesus and his work was increasing, my relationship with my wife was going in the opposite direction. Tension in our family and my in-laws was growing, our son Carl was about 6 years old, and we realized we needed time apart. Space to take a breath and recuperate. My brother by this time had made his mark in the entertainment scene in Canada and by 1979 had become a huge star. He suggested we live with him and his wife for a while in Toronto to help my wife and I get back on track. I left for Canada in June 1979 and realize now just how much a blessing it was for both my wife and me. I set up my own business painting and decorating and within five months had laid a foundation and a great future for my family in Canada. I returned to Wales in October with the intention of taking my family and starting a new life. We went through the immigration process and looked forward to a new life in a new country, but, even though we could make our plans, it is God that ultimately orders our steps.

While in the final stages of the process, I received a phone call from the job centre in *Resolven*. I was now living in *Glynneath*, a dizzy five miles away from my hometown. They were inviting me to apply for a job in the local YMCA. The club was on the point of closure with only a handful of members. They were offering employment for four out of work Youth workers for one year to resurrect interest in the club. I told them of my plans to emigrate to Canada, but they insisted I at least come for the interview. I had nothing to lose. I wouldn't get the job anyway. My disinterest would do the work for me. Little did I know God was setting me up, He was about to ambush me with His plan predestined even before I was born. Yes! They offered me the job. I couldn't rest for days. I was torn between what I thought was His plan for my future –

Canada – with what I was now beginning to realize was the real plan – *Resolven*. I went with His plan, and took the job, not realizing God was manoeuvring me into a position to launch me into a ministry which has grown and developed to this present day.

The employment was only for one year, but we saw not only the youth club revive into a busy, thriving, healthy place for young people's recreation but also God used me to reach many of those young people with the Gospel, many of them receiving Christ and going on to make something of their lives. Then, one day, my life was about to change forever – God was about to ambush me again. A young man came to me one night at the club and asked me to come to his school in Swansea to speak and sing to the students during their morning assembly.

'I've cleared it with the headmaster' he said, 'please will you come?'

This was a first for me! I could only play two 'Christian songs' on my guitar, and I was certain they would be totally irrelevant to those teenagers my young friend was asking me to speak and sing to. He assured me they would love it. I agreed, went to the school, sang and spoke at the morning assembly and walked off stage to the echoing sound of my own steps. I wanted to find a place to hide for the rest of my life. It was a disaster. At least I thought it was. During the whole fifteen minutes, (which felt like fifteen years) they just looked at me as if I was some experiment the school had decided to exhibit to explain the Missing Link. There was no outward response to my singing or speaking – just a look of scared amazement. I was scheduled to do it all again at a lunch time session in the gym. The realization of having to go through that all again aroused emotions in me somewhat like a condemned man awaiting execution. Then, I comforted myself believing, no one will turn up anyway after what they just experienced. I walked into the gym at 12.55 and thought I'd come to the wrong place, it was packed! I went through the exact same routine as the morning again with the same response. It's as though they'd paid money to come and see the eighth Wonder of the World. I asked them to bow their eyes and close their heads! (That's how nervous I was).

I made an appeal for them to receive Christ and to my amazement over fifty percent of them responded. The headmaster was so blown away he arranged with the Youth Club to allow me to stay the whole week to share my faith in Christ. Revival broke out in that school and set the scene for what God had planned for me and for the next eight years of my life. Again, I had made my plans believing it was under God's direction because of my rapport with young people I now believed God was calling me to be a schoolteacher. So, I went to the local teacher training college and applied for entry. I will never forget sitting there being interviewed by 3 pompous professors explaining to me that entry was impossible in my case. They told me I was in desperate need of further education qualifications, which, they emphasized, was impossible for me to attain because it would take two years to study the courses necessary to achieve the standard required for entry.

'Mr. Bevan', one of the professors said, looking at me over his half-rimmed glasses, 'the entry date to enrol in this college is in nine months and the qualifications you need to enter will take you two years, and that's if you pass!' Then, leaning forward condescendingly, he said, 'I was visiting the hospital the other day and saw there was a vacancy for a porter, why don't you apply for that job?'

I wanted to forget everything Jesus had taught me about loving your enemy at that point! But I restrained myself and blurted out very confidently that I would be back in nine months with the necessary qualifications for entry into the college. I walked out with the determination to return victorious even if it was just to prove those naysayers wrong. Armed with a study plan that bordered on the lifestyle of a hermit, my chosen subjects of study: English and Religious Education, I gave myself to it. After nine months of life in the academic trenches, I emerged with a B in both subjects and couldn't wait to return to those professors to wave my medals of valour in their faces.

But God was about to ambush me again. I had made my plans, but He was about to order my steps. It was a Tuesday night; I'm sitting in our weekly prayer meeting. The following morning, I'm expecting to be standing in front of those professors waving my newly acquired qualifications at their noses. They were my passport to what I believed to be the plan of God for the next season of my life. But it was not a normal Tuesday night. On this occasion, we had a group of young fireballs sharing their vision about reaching thousands for Jesus using a three thousand-seater circus tent. They were passionate, even radical, in their approach, especially in their use of music to reach the masses. And they had my full attention. Their passion inspired me, and their vision captivated me. Suddenly, I was ambushed. *You're going to join this team.* I knew full well who was speaking. His words were as clear as a bell. So, I began to have an internal 'reasoning with the Lord', reminding Him of the intense study over the past year, the favour He had given me to communicate to young people, the interview the following morning to enter teaching training college. Quietly He whispered again, *I know, I was preparing you for this – not that.* I now realize that study period was used by God to create a love in my heart for reading, writing and meditating, disciplines I would need especially during the twenty-five years of pastoring the same Church. I sat there stunned, amazed, excited and ambushed. I had made my plans but again, God was ordering my steps. I returned home that night and told my wife what had happened. She looked at me, said nothing, but the look said it all. 'He's off on one again'. The phone rang, it was one of the team who had been in Church that night.

'Ray, this is Robert. We were at your Church tonight. We've heard about your work with young people, and we all feel that you should be part of our team. What do you think?' So, for the next two years, I joined the circus. Well, at least the circus tent. The team was called International Outreach, and with family and team members we were about twenty-nine people in total. Through that ministry we saw thousands come to Christ. During those two years, we also spent five months touring Spain. I cannot tell you the lessons I learnt during those years. The stories and testimonies of God's Grace sustaining and providing for us. At one time, whilst ministering in Spain, finances got so thin we resorted to frying potato peelings for our food. They actually taste great on toast! Two members of that team are now ministering with Hillsong Church; Robert Fergusson, one of their teachers and Steve Dixon, the campus Pastor for Hillsong Brisbane.

Towards the end of that two years, this would be about 1982, we all felt we had completed what God wanted us to do and went our separate ways. We returned as a family to *Glyn Neath*, South Wales and I was fully prepared to resurrect my painting and decorating business until God gave me further instruction. During those days, (I was by now thirty-two), I still struggled with inferiority, insecurity and a host of other emotional giants so when I felt God say to me '*What you did for the past two years was preparation for the next season of your life*'. I felt the Lord was asking me to continue reaching young people in schools and Churches through music and testimony. The problem was, I had no band to back me up and no invitations to minister anywhere. So, I told the Lord 'There is the phone, there is the letterbox, wherever you send me I will go.' I was so fearful of stepping out into ministry alone, I wanted to make it as hard for God as possible! But nothing is impossible with God.

The phone started to ring, the invitations began to arrive so armed with my little PA system, a few backing tracks and a guitar on which I could now play four songs, I pushed out from the shore. For the next seven years, the Holy Spirit filled those fragile sails and blew me into the most amazing season of my life. It would take another book just to record the miracles God performed during that time. Oh, I forgot to mention that when I joined International Outreach, I hadn't really sung seriously since I left the Jaguars, and even during the 60's, it was my brother that had the voice, not me. So, when the team of International Outreach, asked me to sing backing vocals on their album, I told them, I really didn't have a strong voice. We went to the studio to record the album. I was filled with trepidation, even at the thought of singing backing vocals, I didn't want to disappoint the team. On arrival at the studio, the team leader turned to me and said, (I was about to be ambushed again), 'Ray, the Holy Spirit has told me, you are to sing lead on all the songs.'

I wanted to run and hide! I'd heard the songs, I would never be able to reach some of those high notes, so I said 'no, youv'e got it wrong, I haven't got that strong a voice or that big a range'.

'Well, just try' he said. I walked into the vocal recording booth and what happened next took my breath away. I started to sing, and this voice came out of my mouth I'd never heard before. I thought I was listening to someone else sing. It truly was supernatural. God gifted me with a voice that day and He has used, and still is using, nine albums later, to bless countless thousands. I still receive testimonies of people who tell me, how through the songs, has helped them through times of devastating tragedy and unbearable pain. My singing ministry is again a wonderful testimony to 'Grace Alone'. And so, for the next seven years, God used me to reach multiple thousands of young people in schools and Churches all over the UK and even a five-week tour of California working with Nicky Cruz, the main character in the classic book '*The Cross and the Switchblade*'.

Sometimes I would perform as many as thirty concerts a week. When people asked me how I maintained that level of intensity, consistency and passion over those seven years, my answer is 'Grace Alone'. From the troubled streets of Northern Ireland during the early 1980's to the ghettos of San Francisco; From hard lined prisons like Strangeways in Manchester to Tia Juana; From ministering to five people in a house group to thousands on the shores of Lisbon, Portugal with Reinhardt Bonnke, I saw the power of God released through 'Grace Alone'. Through someone who simply said, 'I'm available, there's the phone, there's the letterbox'. God is not really interested in your ability, but your *availability.*

In 1989 God was about to ambush me again. I'd felt we had to relocate from our small Welsh village to a place that would give me easier access to the motorways and airports. So, in 1982, we moved to Newport, South Wales, the last city before entering England. From 1982 to 1989 this was to be the base of operations. We attended a local Pentecostal Church in that city. I was experiencing a growing frustration. At the invitation of local Churches, I would spend a week ministering in the schools in their area, then inviting the young people to the Church at the end of the week for a concert. Many hundreds were brought to Christ using this method. I remember after ministering for three days in Newry, Northern Ireland, during those troubled days, five-hundred young people responded at the concert, both Catholic and Protestant. It was quite miraculous considering the culture of hate and violence. In Manchester, after visiting five schools, the effect of the Gospel was so powerful, the five headmasters each offered me a job. When I asked why, they said, since my visit, bullying, drug abuse, and a whole host of negative behaviour had been seriously affected for the better. I didn't take the jobs but was infused with more passion in my confidence of Grace Alone. But here lay my frustration. The young people were receiving Jesus by Grace Alone, then being introduced to churches which preached law. Grace to receive Salvation and law to maintain it. Although hundreds of young people were responding to the Gospel, the Churches that invited me could not keep them, it was so annoying, and I'd thought all my effort to reach these young people was futile if there wasn't a place where they could grow.

By now, I was attending a new Church in Newport called The King's Church. It seemed the leadership understood my dilemma and wanted to use me to reach the youth of our city. I was so thrilled to find such a home for my family and base for my ministry. One Saturday night, I arranged a concert and over one thousand young people showed up. Many found Christ and started attending the Church, but things were about to turn horribly sour. The two leaders that were leading the Church started to introduce some membership criteria that were very controlling and along with that, they saw me as a threat to the way that they wanted to run the Church and asked me to leave. I pleaded with them and reassured them I only wanted to serve them to reach the lost. But jealousy in a leader's heart can have a devastating effect so out I went. During this time, I could really relate to David who only wanted to serve Saul but instead of being appreciated, he was persecuted all because of ministerial jealousy.

I was really concerned for the Church fellowship and a leadership that simply wanted control and unbiblical submission. I gave myself to prayer every morning and went on my prayer walk where God began to give me insight as to which spirits were working through these two leaders. It would take another book to explain that season of warfare but it's enough to say I started to come against the spiritual wickedness that sought to bind God's people. During that season of prayer, God gave me some incredible revelation from the story of raising Lazarus from the dead. I wrote it all down and prepared six messages with the revelation I received. For an evangelist, six messages can last ten years! Little did I know, God was setting me up for another ambush.

My telephone rang. It was one of the trustees of the building where the church congregated. The building was used previously as a roller-skating disco and had the potential to be transformed into a one-thousand-seater auditorium; which, after 30 years of renovation, it now is. I remember standing at the back of the hall one day, looking at the dark, painted walls with grotesque images painted all over them. I remember thinking at the time, 'This would be a great place for a church.' Little did I realize that dream would become a reality and God would use *me* to bring it to pass.

"Have you heard?" The trustee asked,

"Heard what?" I replied. He told me there had been a massive upheaval in the church. The two leaders had gone their separate ways. Both left the premises with their particular group of people following them and the remaining Trustees were left holding the bill for the mortgage payments.

"Why are you calling *me*," I asked?

"Well," he said, "a small group of people still believe there should be a church in this building and after speaking to them the only one they would trust to lead them is you. Will you take on the responsibility?"

I was stunned but somehow not surprised. During my time of prayer for the situation, I realized God was not only using me in prayer but preparing me for leadership. The revelation He gave me from the raising of Lazarus from the dead would be the seed from which a strong vibrant church would grow.

The church split had made the front page of our local newspaper. Details about what had happened (including the violence involved) were recorded in black and white and read by thousands of people in our city. The split put a bad taste in the mouth of those we were trying to reach for the gospel, and, like the story of Lazarus, the situation had gone from difficult to impossible. The church, like the body in the tomb, was dead and stinking. I put the phone down and remembered gazing out of my study window and asking God a simple question: 'Is this another Ambush?' Immediately I felt a stirring in my spirit. The only way to describe it was like the sun rising on a cold, frosty morning flooding the whole landscape with brilliant light. Then He gently reminded me of the six sermons He had given me during those months of prayer.

If you follow the principles that I used to raise Lazarus from the dead and use them in this situation you will see the church walk out of its tomb and people will come from miles to see the wonder of the miracle.

I argued with God over my credentials to step into an Apostolic role, but He encouraged me by reassuring me. He showed me that my lack of experience would be to my advantage. He reminded me of Noah's lack of experience to build something he had never seen, and He told me that my lack of experience would force me to depend upon His instruction, as I too was being asked to build something I had never seen.

Armed with a call from God and six sermons, I turned up that first Sunday morning on June 10th, 1989 to find thirty confused, hurting but trusting believers who, unknowingly, were about to be ambushed by the grace of God. My insecurities were running rampant and I told God that I would give it six weeks because I only had six sermons! I even travelled the country trying to find someone else, someone with the qualifications and desire to take on the church. Finally, I realized it was me who had been ambushed and chosen for the task ahead. Six weeks turned into twenty-five years.

Paul the apostle, in his immortal words, encapsulates the secret to my journey after this very point after being ambushed by grace time and time again. 'I am what I am by the grace of God'. Throughout this book I will share with you the lessons, heart breaks, the joys and miracles I have been graced to endure and enjoy. My confidence to do what He has called me to do, is His confidence in me to do it.

And it's all because I'm 'Graced' and so are you.

CHAPTER THREE

GRACE FOR SELFISHNESS

It's a Saturday night in 1960, I'm 11 years of age sitting in my living room with my two brothers, my sister, my dog Kim and my ancient one-toothed cat named Tibs. It's around 11.30pm and we're all huddled, bleary-eyed, around our black and white TV watching Elliott Ness in the Untouchables. Why would our mother allow us to stay up that late you may ask? Good question! The answer – she's out working at one of her four jobs to help pay for the upkeep of six people, a dog and a one-toothed cat. However, that doesn't excuse our bed-time training. Surely we should have put ourselves to bed. Surely our mother, you are thinking, would be angry when she came home and found us bed skiving, watching gangster movies. That may be true on any other night but not Saturdays. Our excuse for staying up late is not our passion for late night movies, but pies, fish, chicken and chips. You see my mother's Saturday night job was working in the local fish and chip shop. Not the 'glamorous' job of cooking and serving, but the finger-numbing chore of peeling the potatoes, by hand.

I will never forget my mother's hands. You could sandpaper a door with them in readiness for painting. Sometimes they were so abused from scrubbing floors, washing clothes, carrying coal for our open fire and peeling hundreds of potatoes she could hardly hold a spoon to stir her tea. Sometimes I noticed they were so cracked and sore it looked like she had punched into a bucket of broken glass for an hour. My mother's hands. But what has my mother's hands have to do with four kids staying up late on a Saturday night? Well, it was the expectation of what those hands would be carrying home after a hard night's graft. Rather than throw out what didn't sell, the owner of the fish shop would allow my mum to take home what was left unsold. Sometimes it would only be a few pies, sausage rolls and a plateful of chips, but who knows, tonight, there could be a battered cod and my favourite 'deep fried chicken'. It was that level of expectation that kept us awake, not Elliott Ness gunning down some villain.

At 11.45pm, the door opened, and we could smell the amazing aroma of fish and chips long before we saw our mum. She wearily dumped the large newspaper wrapped package on the table, spilling its mouth-watering contents everywhere. The vinegar-soaked chips were piled higher than usual – we were in for a feast tonight. There were at least four pies, a couple of sausage rolls, and one large piece of battered cod but… no chicken. What! No chicken! But chicken is my favourite, my mother knows that! Surely, she could have asked the owner to throw one in, even though there was none left over. How inconsiderate of my mother. I voiced my disappointment to my mum as only a selfish eleven-year-old could. There was no rebuke, no withholding of what was actually available, just a tired look of disappointment at my lack of gratitude. Years later, while preparing a message on the power of gratitude, I asked the Holy Spirit to give me an illustration that would encapsulate the essence of a grateful heart. The incident I just described to you, was what the Holy Spirit accessed from my childhood memory. I asked Him what the relevance was. He simply said *'Your mother's hands'*. He said, *'You were more concerned that there was no chicken in the vinegar-soaked newspaper than the cracked bleeding hands that were holding them'*. I was stunned into silence as I realized just how ungratefully selfish the human heart could be, especially when it comes to our relationship with Jesus. How many times have I wallowed in self-pity an ungratefulness towards Jesus because my prayers and His answers don't match? When my expectation and His silence cause me to have an eleven-year-old rant at his seeming indifference to my situation. How often do I despise what's been graced to me and totally overlooked the nail scarred hands that were skewered to a Roman killing post to give them to me?

Timothy Keller in his amazing book on marriage gives incredible insight into the destructive power of selfishness in the marriage relationship. In fact, the cancer of selfishness spreads its venom, poisoning all productive relationships. The main barrier to the development of a selfless servant is the radical self-centeredness of the human heart. Self-centeredness is a havoc-wreaking problem in many relationships in the Church, in marriage, and in family. It is the cancer at the centre of disunity and contention. According to the Apostle Paul, love is the very opposite of self-seeking and the only antidote to this killer virus. *Love is patient and kind; it does not envy or boast it's neither proud or rude and never self-seeking. It is not easily angered and keeps no record of wrongs (1 Corinthians 13:4-5).* Self-centeredness is easily seen in the signs Paul lists. Impatience; irritability; lack of grace; unkindness of speech; Envious broodings on the better situations of others; Holding past injuries and hurts against others. Self-centeredness by its very character makes you blind to your own whilst being hypersensitive, offended and angered by that of others. The result is always a downward spiral into self-pity, anger, and despair as relationships all around you get eaten away to nothing.

There are many reasons why we cannot see our own selfishness, one of the main factors that hides us is our own history of mistreatment. Many people are straight jacketed by hurt. Hurt by parents, former spouses and Church leadership. They live chained by woundedness causing them to be so self-absorbed that the development of a grateful heart is virtually impossible. When you begin to talk to wounded people it's not long before they begin talking about themselves. They are so engrossed in their own pain and problems that they don't realize what it looks like to other people. They are incapable of being sensitive to the needs of other people, they don't pick up the clues of those who are hurting or if they do, they only do it in a self-absorbed way, that is, they do so with a view of helping to rescue them in order to feel better about themselves. They get involved with others in an obsessive, controlling way because they're actually meeting their own needs. Totally deceiving themselves regarding their condition. When you point out selfish behaviour to a wounded person, he or she will say 'well maybe so, but you don't understand what it's like.' The wounds justify the behaviour.

There are two ways to diagnose and treat this condition – The secular way and the Gospel way. Secularists say that if people are self-absorbed and mess up it is because they lack self-esteem so we should encourage them to be good to themselves, to live for themselves and not others. In this view of things, we give wounded people almost nothing but support, encouraging them to stop letting others rule their lives, urging them to find out what their dreams are and take steps to fulfil them. That is, we think, the way to healing. But this approach assumes that self-centeredness isn't natural that it is only the product of some kind of mistreatment. However, this view of things, simply doesn't work. It is impossible to have a smooth-running relationship with people who always feel that his or her desires should have pre-eminence because of all he or she has been through in life. The Gospel approach begins with a different analysis of the situation. It tells us that as badly wounded as people may be, the resulting self-absorption of the human heart was not caused by mistreatment it was only magnified and shaped by it. Their mistreatment simply poured oil on the fire and the flame and smoke now choke them, but their self-centeredness already existed prior to their woundedness. Therefore, if you do nothing but urge people to look out for number one, you will be setting them up for future failure in any relationship.

Paul's description of the power of the Gospel totally demolishes that secular view on how to deal with self-centeredness:

2 Corinthians 5:15 *'And he died for all, that those who live should no longer live for themselves but for Him who died for them and was raised again'*

All of us must be challenged to see that our self-centredness has not been caused by the people who hurt us, it's only been aggravated by the abuse. We must do something about it, or we will live miserable lives. Jesus' words in Matthew 16:25 cut across the secular antidote for self-centredness and declares the key to deliverance from this merciless prison is not to look in but to look out. It's not to save our life, but to lose it. He is in fact saying, 'if your personal happiness is more important to you than gratefully acknowledging what I did for you and in turn passing on unselfish love to others then you will eat the fruit of a miserable life'.

On the other hand, if, in all things, you give thanks, the outflow of a grateful heart is always generosity. The outflow of a grateful heart will always produce a harvest of unselfishness in your life, overflowing and gushing into the lives of others. God's answer to the onslaught of selfishness that clamours and fights for pre-eminence in our lives is Grace Alone.

CHAPTER FOUR

GRACE FOR SUFFERING

During a ministry trip to America, our children's grandparents were arriving from Norway to look after them while we were away. We left for the USA with excited, contented hearts, knowing God's blessing was on us and ahead of us and the children would be safe and cared for in the hands of their grandparents. The trip went well, and, on our return, we found three happy kids and two tired grandparents. We thanked them for their help, said our goodbyes and they left for the airport. It was a Saturday, and we were jet lagged from our trip and needed an early night. I wanted to be well rested in order to greet Sunday morning with energy and passion to preach to a hungry congregation. I slept well, rose early, meditated on my message for that morning, had a cup of coffee, got dressed and went to Church. The service was wonderful, and it was one of those Sundays where I experienced a liberating freedom as I preached God's word. One of the contributing factors I'm sure, was the new very comfortable underwear I had put on that morning. I remember thinking I will have to buy some more of these shorts, they're amazing.

When I arrived home that morning, the first thing I did was to check where I'd bought this wonderful new underwear. Then I realized. They were not mine. I should have sussed that out when I realized the elastic came nearly up to my neck. It was then the horrific revelation hit me – I was wearing Granny's knickers! She must have left them in the bedroom during their stay at our house. I don't know whether this would be classed as a sin, but I was preaching God's Word wearing women's underwear! They were the most comfortable underwear I'd ever worn. The thought came to me – perhaps it was Holy Spirit inspired? *'Ray, – just because it's comfortable, doesn't make it right'.* And then immediately, He flipped the coin and said *'Ray, just because it's uncomfortable, doesn't make it wrong.'* Some of you reading these words, may be experiencing the most uncomfortable season of your life and as a result, questioning your position regarding the will of God for you. Why is this happening to me? Is God judging me for some sin or bad decision? Surely, the safest place is in the will of God? One thing I've learnt is that the safest place is definitely in the will of God, but it may not necessarily mean it's the most comfortable.

If obeying God is rational, and always reasonable, then David should have left Goliath alone. Hosea should never have married a prostitute and what was Moses thinking when he pointed his staff at the Red Sea? The language of God's will for those who will follow his leadings, can sometimes sound insane. Anyone who risks listening to God and following His voice, knows that to everyone who is deaf to His voice, your actions will seem that you've gone crazy.

The most comfortable place is in the will of God – really? Tell that to Stephen who was stoned after his first sermon. Or Matthew who was stabbed to death in Persia. What about Mark and Thomas who were torn apart by horses. Luke was hanged. Peter and Philip were crucified. Bartholomew was skinned alive and both Mathias and Paul were beheaded. Often, God does not remove you from a dark place to accommodate your comfort but on the contrary, it's to supply grace for you to light up the darkness for His glory. The Apostle Paul came to the realization of the power of God's grace in uncomfortable places.

To see a real grace-based joy, give it the pain of persecution. To see a real grace-based faith, give it an onslaught of fear. To see a real grace-based peace, give it a storm to unsettle it. To see a real grace-based courage, give it a Goliath to challenge it. To see a real grace-based call, give it a Pharaoh to oppose it. To see a real grace-based love, give it a cross to kill it. To see a real grace-based long-suffering, give it prolonged frustration.

The most amazing demonstration of this truth came from the lips of the Apostle Paul as he battled with the confusion of doing the will of God, and at the same time, trying to unravel the mystery of personal suffering through persecution. If you were writing a resumé to a potential employer, what areas of your life would you highlight? Obviously, you would present yourself in the most positive way possible. You would list your work record along with the glowing references of your amazing abilities, meticulous integrity and your wonderful sunshine personality that will add strength to the team. The Apostle Paul on one occasion was challenged to present his resumé proving his authenticity as a minister of the Gospel. Wow! What an opportunity to gather all the testimonies of all those who had been blessed through his teaching and healing ministry, not forgetting his unique encounter with the risen Jesus and the spellbinding details of his visit to Heaven. He had so many amazing experiences to present to his critics to validate his calling. In 2 Corinthians 12, he did mention his visit to Heaven and the manifestations of miraculous signs and wonders that should accompany an Apostle's calling, but he was careful not to amplify that side of his ministry. His validation came down firmly on the side of his hardships.

> *If I wanted to boast, I would be no fool in doing so, because I would be telling the truth. But I won't do it, because I don't want anyone to give me credit beyond what they can see in my life or hear in my message, even though I have received such wonderful revelations from God. So to keep me from becoming proud, I was given a thorn in my flesh, a messenger from Satan to torment me and keep me from becoming proud. Three different times I begged the Lord to take it away. Each time he said, "My grace is all you need. My power works best in weakness." So now I am glad to boast about my weaknesses, so that the power of Christ can work through me. That's why I take pleasure in my weaknesses, and in the insults, hardships, persecutions, and troubles that I suffer for Christ. For when I am weak, then I am strong.* 2 Corinthians, 12:6-10 New Living Translation

To shut the mouths of his critics, as they demanded proof of his calling, he simply took his shirt off and showed them what it had already cost him;

> *From now on let no one trouble me, for I bear in my body the marks of the Lord Jesus...* Galatians, 6:17 New King James Version

Graced to validate his calling, Paul did not present his triumphs but his troubles. He did not boast about his successes but his sufferings. In fact, this is what Jesus declared over him at his ordination in Acts 9:15-16 (in italics);

'For Paul is My chosen vessel...' (Yeah! – did you hear that? Don't mess with me! I'm chosen, I'm special, a celebrity)

'...to take My message to the gentiles...' (wow! What a life I have in front of me, travelling the world, promised success by Jesus – bring it on!)

'...and kings...' (can this get any better? I'm going to rub shoulders with royalty, my friends and peers will stand in awe as well as the people of Israel, kings, unbelieving nations, how am I going to contain myself from the adulation and personal invites)

'...and I will show him how much he must suffer for Me' (uh, oh.. that part doesn't seem to fit in with the rest of my resume – must be a mistake. Suffering? That doesn't fit in with my idea of a successful ministry!)

I wonder how we as ministers would respond to the challenge to validate our calling, would it be the size of our Church? The busyness of our diary? A list of all the documented miracles as a result of our anointing? I think Paul's example is a sober reminder regarding the foundation for our boasting. His grace, not our glory; His strength in our weakness; His triumph through our trials; His success through our suffering.

Rick Renner, in his book, *If You Were God Would You Choose You?* (Rick Renner Ministries, 2000) describes in detail the list of Paul's sufferings as recorded in 2 Corinthians 11. As I read them, I felt my pathetic complaints regarding my own trials melt like snow on the fire in comparison with what he endured. In fact, reading them silenced me into an embarrassing admission of selfishness. As I recalled the times I have complained to God about my own trials in the ministry. Let's read the list and be humbled:

> *Are they ministers of Christ? – I speak as a fool – I am more: in labours more abundant, in stripes above measure, in prisons more frequently, in deaths often. From the Jews five times I received forty stripes minus one. Three times I was beaten with rods; once I was stoned; three times I was shipwrecked; a night and a day I have been in the deep; in journeys often, in perils of waters, in perils of robbers, in perils of my own countrymen, in perils of the Gentiles, in perils in the city, in perils in the wilderness, in perils in the sea, in perils among false brethren; in weariness and toil, in sleeplessness often, in hunger and thirst, in fasting's often, in cold and nakedness – besides the other things, what comes upon me daily: my deep concern for all the churches. Who is weak, and I am not weak? Who is made to stumble, and I do not burn with indignation? If I must boast, I will boast in the things which concern my infirmity.*
> 2 Corinthians 11:23-30 New King James Version

He gave them a 'head's up in 1 Corinthians 4:10-13 (NKJV)

> *We are fools for Christ's sake, but you are wise in Christ! We are weak, but you are strong! You are distinguished, but we are dishonoured! To the present hour we both hunger and thirst, and we are poorly clothed, and beaten, and homeless. And we labour, working with our own hands. Being reviled, we bless; being persecuted, we endure; being defamed, we entreat. We have been made as the filth of the world, the offscouring of all things until now.*

But now he is forced to go into detail to silence the mouths of his critics. The Amplified translation of 2 Corinthians 11:30 reads *'if I MUST boast I will boast in the things that show my infirmity, the things by which I am made weak and contemptable in the eyes of my opponents'.* (Emphasis added)

The NLT reads, *'if I MUST boast, I would rather boast about the things that show how weak I am'* (Emphasis added)

And then Paul goes on to list an incredible array of personal suffering that glorifies God and magnifies His grace in a way his successes never could. When I read them, I thought how anyone would not only survive in these things but thrive in them? How could Paul do what he did in the face of such horrific suffering? The answer, of course, is 'The Grace of God'. And that was Paul's intention – not to throw the spotlight on his achievements but on the grace of God. 'In labours more abundant' the Greek words used to describe his labour in the Gospel could be translated like this *'I worked more abundantly than most men'.* Or, *'I worked more than you can ever begin to comprehend'.* In other words, Paul declares when it comes to hard work, no one is a harder worker than I am. *'In stripes above measure'* the word stripes in the Greek language 'to violently strike', it's the same word used by Jesus in the parable of the Good Samaritan. Luke 10:30 Jesus says the robbers wounded him and departed leaving him half dead. The word implies a mortal wound. This is the word Paul uses. He says, 'I have been beaten to the point of death and not only that, but with *stripes above measure'.* A beating way over the top. Beyond the range of anything considered normal. This word 'above measure' in the Greek is *hyperberballo,* from where we get the word *hyperbole,* meaning, 'over the top'. It not only describes the intensity of the beatings, but also the frequency. What Paul's enemies did to his body was way over the top.

'In prisons more frequent' 'prison' in the Greek – a place heavily guarded by keepers. Usually, a small dark chamber in which the most hardened, dangerous prisoners were confined. Paul was kept in this type of extreme confinement many times during his ministry; sometimes for years. *'In deaths often'* Paul constantly lived with the physical threat of death. I remember some years ago when I lived for a short time under that threat – the fear of it was more debilitating than any attack. When Paul wrote *'I die daily',* 1 Corinthians 15:31, he meant 'I am constantly confronted with the prospect of death daily'. *'Five times I received forty stripes save one'.* This was a Jewish method of punishment applied to Paul on five separate occasions!

> *...then it shall be, if the wicked man deserves to be beaten, that the judge will cause him to lie down and be beaten in his presence, according to his guilt, with a certain number of blows. Forty blows he may give him and no more, lest he should exceed this and beat him with many blows above these, and your brother be humiliated in your sight.* Deuteronomy 25:2-3 NKJV.

This was one of the most vicious punishments of the ancient world. This type of horrific beating left permanent scars on the body. The first third of the lashes were across the upper chest and face. The remaining two thirds were applied to the back, buttocks and legs. The victim was forced to bend over to make it easier for the torturer to hit the body. The whip was made of three cords. Paul received thirty-nine lashes, that meant one hundred and seventeen lashes at each beating. He went through this gruelling torture on five different occasions which means five-hundred and eighty-five lashes were laid across Paul's upper chest, face, back, buttocks and legs. There wasn't a place on his body that hadn't been beaten or had pieces of flesh ripped out.

To one group, as I have already mentioned, as they questioned his authenticity as a minister of the Gospel, he simply showed them those marks. Authority is not what you know, it's what you've survived.

'*Thrice was I beaten with rods.*' In the ancient world, a beating with rods was an ugly, horrible form of torture. A person's body was bound tightly then hoisted in the air by his feet. While hanging upside down the torturer would beat the victims' feet with a metal rod. At times, the beating was so severe that the victim would never walk again. It's obvious, the devil hated Paul's feet as he preached the Gospel of peace because, according to God, they are beautiful.

> *How beautiful upon the mountains*
> *Are the feet of him who brings good news,*
> *Who proclaims peace,*
> *Who brings glad tidings of good things,*
> *Who proclaims salvation,*
> *Who says to Zion, "Your God reigns!"*
> Isaiah 52:7 (NKJV)

This vicious attack on Paul's feet was an indication of how much the devil hates and fears the Gospel.

'*Once I was stoned*'. This event occurred in Acts 14:19 after a successful campaign amongst the Gentiles in Lystra, Jewish opponents came from Iconium to stir up trouble for Paul. They were so effective in distributing bad information, the entire city turned against him, stoned him and left him for dead. Stoning was a malicious act to ensure the victims death. Stoning did not usually stop until the head was crushed. When it was apparent that there was no possibility of survival, the corpse was dragged out of the city and left for dog food. Acts 14:20 says the disciples came prayed for Paul and *'he rose up'*. I believe that this describes a resurrection not a healing. He was stoned to death. What a wonderful demonstration of the power of Grace. Paul declared *'His grace is made perfect in weakness'*. Well! You can't get weaker than dead. God's resurrection grace kicked in when Paul was at his weakest. At Paul's weakest moment, he experienced grace in its essence. He told the Corinthian people in 2 Corinthians 12:1-4 of a visit he made to Heaven. He explained he heard and saw things that he had never been given permission to speak about (unlike many books written today regarding Heavenly visits). When did Paul make his visit to Heaven? Could it have been at Lystra? I personally think so.

The amazing thing is, even after such an horrific attack, he got up, dusted himself down and went back into the city! The next day, he left on a long walking trip to Derbe; a distance of about 30 miles. What! He was stoned to death the day before. When I get 'man flu', I'm in bed for days, unable to pull myself out of bed even to make myself food. What has the devil got to do to stop this guy? The act of stoning to death obviously had no debilitating effect on Paul's body, he was able, on the same day, to get up, walk back into the city and then, after a nights' sleep, get up and walk 30 miles the following day! It's no wonder he declared *'The same spirit that raised Jesus from the dead, quicken your mortal body'*. *'Three times I suffered shipwreck'*. Paul's life reads like James Bond; you just can't kill him.

Only one of Paul's shipwrecks is recorded in the New Testament, in Acts 27. That was horrific enough. During that whole experience, he was threatened with murder, drowning, received a venomous snake bite and met with a hostile population on the island of Malta. In addition to that shipwreck, Paul testifies to have been shipwrecked on two other occasions *'a night and day in the deep'*. That phrase 'a night and day' refers to a twenty-four-hour time period of floating aimlessly in an open ocean.

'In journeys often'. In the Greek it often means a walking journey. Using your concordance, look up the word *'walked'* through the book of Acts and be amazed of how much of Paul's ministry was conducted on foot. Keep in mind, the man who did this walking was the same man who

had his feet beaten with metal rods on three occasions. Paul must have enjoyed a healthy body. A sick man could never accomplish such physical exertions in the face of such physical torture. I believe, Paul knew how to draw upon Christ's resurrection power to keep him strong and healthy.

'In perils' Paul uses this word eight times regarding water, robbers, his own countrymen and the heathen; in cities, the wilderness, in the sea and among false brethren. The word *peril* means extremely dangerous and volatile situations. In short, Paul was saying 'I have been in extremely dangerous, volatile situations as I've sought to carry the Gospel'. He crossed rivers, watched out for robbers and then he itemized more emotional, mental and physical threats he had to endure in the process of outworking his calling. *'I get weary'*, he declares, *'because of the hard work involved in what I'm called to do. In watching often sometimes I have sleepless nights while journeying along bandit lined roads. I've often been hungry and thirsty as we've run out of food and water sometimes. In fasting often sometimes unconsciously because I'm more concerned about preaching and teaching my hearers I just forget to eat and sometimes I fast deliberately to sharpen my spiritual senses to God's voice. My prison stints have often been brutally hard, not just the beatings and the isolation but sometimes stripped naked to sleep on the stone-cold floors in the worst possible conditions* 'and on top of all that he concludes *'I have the burden of all the Churches'. I pray for them, write to them, long to visit them and live with the constant frustration that I can't speak with them.* Paul said, *why do I boast about all these hardships? Because I want to declare to men and demons nobody could survive all this without supernatural help.* Paul is encouraging us to understand that God's grace operates fully and is made perfect in weakness. Paul doesn't hide the fact that this revelation was discovered after three desperate pleas for God to make his life easier.

> *If I wanted to boast, I would be no fool in doing so, because I would be telling the truth. But I won't do it, because I don't want anyone to give me credit beyond what they can see in my life or hear in my message, even though I have received such wonderful revelations from God. So, to keep me from becoming proud, I was given a thorn in my flesh, a messenger from Satan to torment me and keep me from becoming proud.*
> 2 Corinthians 12:6-8 New Living Translation

These were the words spoken to a man who had had enough; to a man who had reached his limit of endurance. A man who had come to the end of himself. He was tired and confused as to why God was allowing such merciless attacks on his body, mind and emotions. He had had enough of a relentless season of pain and hardship and trial. He could not understand why God would not make his life easier in order for him to carry the Gospel to the world. Three times he pleaded to God for an easier life. Such was the intensity of the attacks he 'begged' God for their removal. The intensity of the request is paralleled with Jesus' cry to His Father in Gethsemane *'Oh my Father, if it's possible, let this cup pass from me'*.

When Paul begged God for the removal of his persecutions and pain, it was a picture of a man who couldn't take it anymore and wanted out. Have I described where you are right now? Are you going through a season of relentless hardship and trial? Have you come to the end of yourself? Do you feel you can't take it anymore and you want out? Like Paul, you have begged God to bring an end to it. And like Paul, you feel God's answer seems like he doesn't care. What is it you're begging God to deliver you from? And things seem to be getting worse. I'm not talking about sickness or lack, but an out-of-control situation that's causing you pain, persecution from people, perhaps even family. God's answer to Paul was not the reply of an indifferent God but a God who wanted Paul to experience something so powerful it would settle his heart, astound his persecutors and embarrass the devil.

> *And He said to me, "My grace is sufficient for you, for My strength is made perfect in weakness." Therefore, most gladly I will rather boast in my infirmities, that the power of Christ may rest upon me. Therefore I take pleasure in infirmities, in reproaches, in needs, in persecutions, in distresses, for Christ's sake. For when I am weak, then I am strong.*
> 2 Corinthians 12:9-10 New King James Version

He's saying, 'My grace is enough to see you through anything the devil throws at you. My grace is more powerful than any satanic attack, than any debilitating emotion – failure, sin or human deficiency. My grace is made perfect in weakness'. Our discomfort is God's opportunity to display His grace. Our weakness is God's opportunity to display His strength. This revelation revolutionized Paul's thinking concerning his trials and declared 'from now on I'm going to boast about my weakness and the insults, and the hardships, the troubles and the persecutions because when I am weak, that's when I'm strong. That's when the power of Christ can work through me and the glory of Christ rest upon me.

It's God's secret weapon for battle weary dreamers and to discover it, you have to get to a place where you want to give up. The great preacher Spurgeon said *'I kiss the wave that throws me against the rocks of despair and discouragement for it is here I find God's secret weapon to sustain me... His Grace'* (Spurgeon, 1874).

As a result of that revelation, Paul effectively said, 'I'm going to stop bellyaching and start boasting. I'm going to stop my pity party and start a praise party. Why? His Grace is sufficient for me! I'm going to stop focusing on the weakness that hinders me and focus on the grace that helps me. I'm going to stop focusing on Satan coming against me and focus on *'Greater is He that is in me''*.

The world applauds achievement, strength and ability. But God gives grace to the humble and is attracted to the weak. That's why Christianity and Darwinism are diametrically opposed. It's not about the survival of the fittest or strongest but it's all about His grace manifested through the weakest and the lowest. Paul's whole desire is to show us and encourage us that God's power and strength are made perfect and operate the best when it's obvious to all you would never survive without it. If you want to experience God's grace, it kicks in at our worst. You want to experience God's love? It operates best when you are hated. You want to experience God's joy? It flourishes during times of sadness. Living with this revelation I can imagine every time Paul was led to the whipping post or thrown into the darkest hole, he didn't view it as an opposition but an opportunity to declare and experience again, grace demonstrated through weakness. *Just because it's comfortable doesn't make it right and remember, just because it's uncomfortable doesn't make it wrong.* Thanks for leaving your knickers Grandma – it helped me understand the power of His grace in trial.

A final thought of encouragement for those of you whose world has been blasted into disarray and confusion because of the nuclear explosion of sudden tragedy, crisis, pain or loss. Mary the mother of Jesus helps us make sense of what seems like a destiny mess. When the shepherds told Mary what the angels had said to them, did this confirm to her that what seemed to be a mess was God working out his plan? Was the message to the shepherds actually a confirmatory sign for Mary when she was forced by the Romans to travel eighty miles, heavily pregnant, at a time when she would much rather give birth to Jesus at home in Nazareth in comfortable, familiar surroundings, with people she knew supporting her. Had she failed God? Birthing God's dream in a cattle-shed, laying His Son in a feeding trough. This was not how she imagined it would be. She'd been likely rejected by her family and to them and her social network she was a slut and a liar. Her world was turned upside down and she was looking upon Heaven's darling laying in a straw-filled feeding trough, a manger. I wonder, can you relate to Mary? You've obeyed God and things have got worse, not better. Life has become harder, not easier. Friends and family misunderstand you and for some, even rejection is part of the package you have been delivered. Are you like Mary, looking into a manger saying, 'have I missed it?' Take heart, the very thing you feel is an indication that you are out of God's will could actually be a sign that you are slap in the middle of it! Just because it's comfortable doesn't mean it's right, and again, just because it's uncomfortable doesn't mean it's wrong.

I am sure, when Mary heard the report of the shepherds' *the sign will be a manger*', her heart settled with the peace that comes of knowing you are in the centre of God's will. Your adverse circumstance could be your manger. Your relational rejection and persecution could be your manger. Your trial could be God's torchlight. Your suffering, as in Paul's case, could be a sign, not a sorrow and a wonderful opportunity to allow Him to reveal His grace through your vulnerability and weakness and who knows, I could be the shepherd called by God to write this chapter for you as a confirmation that you are in the right place.

CHAPTER FIVE

GRACE FOR THE SOIL – PART 1

A week in Menorca, can't wait. I've been looking forward to this holiday for ages and planning to make the most of every day. The lesson I was about to learn was that you don't prepare your holiday using a preacher's mind-set. When preparing a sermon, the aim is to move from point to point in a coordinated fluid way. Each point carefully studied and presented systematically. One point has to be thoroughly squeezed dry of truth before you move on to the next. Wonderful process for sermon construction, hopeless for holiday planning. As I mentally perused the upcoming week, I was determined that every day would be squeezed dry of its delights:

DAY 1. Relaxation, Orientation and Discovery

DAY 2. Sunbathing.

DAY 3. Shopping.

DAY 4. Snorkelling.

DAY 5. Combination of the first 4 days.

I was excited and ready, what could possibly go wrong? Well, the first thing I should have understood is that you don't do your sunbathing in one day! I found my sunbathing spot discovered from my *recon* on the first day. Got there early and spread my enormous beach towel over already hot sand. I worked out the baking time for various parts of my body and envisioned myself, at the end of the day, walking back to my hotel a golden-tanned Greek God. I sprayed the sun protection oil very sparsely over my body, my thinking was, 'not too much – I need to get my tan in one day'. Mr. Sun beat down on my Welsh bleached body, relishing the opportunity to prove how stupid I was to believe that even though he stood ninety-three million miles away, his smile was only there to bless me. Well, after eight hours of roasting under his thirty-eight degrees smile, that respect was earned. I wasn't tanned, I was cooked! I would have been just about ready for dinner for a remote tribe in some dark corner of the world who loved Welsh rarebit. I couldn't move.

I called my friend to help me up, as I stood to my feet, I heard gasps all around from my horrified holiday company. I was so burnt around my midriff there was a blister forming and circling my waist, my legs were redder than a male ostrich on heat and my face resembled a prisoner who had been slapped in the face for hours under interrogation. Very gently, my concerned friends escorted me back to my hotel room. I lay on my bed like a barbequed starfish. The pain was horrific. Cold towels were gently placed around my waist in an attempt to reverse the swelling of the now inner tube-shaped blister, I looked like the Michelin Man. My friends realizing the cold towel wasn't really doing the job, they began to frantically poor out other suggestions on how to deal with this emergency. One put forward a remedy she read about in a magazine about how to deal with severe sun burn. Heat on heat. The article drew its remedy from some pre-century prescription. The idea was to apply hot water not cold water to the affected area, as hot as you could bare, and apparently it would neutralize the pain. Well! You could hear my screams in Turkey.

For the rest of that day and night I lay in agony on my bed managing only a few hours' sleep. I awoke on the third day realizing my planned holiday was ruined. I had 3 days left and the blister had subsided allowing me enough pain free movement to get up and walk around. It was obvious I couldn't expose my blow torch frame to the sun, so I decided to gently place items of clothing next to my skin which would not cause further irritation. My linen trousers worked perfectly, my cheese cloth shirt was ideal and one of my friends' wives kindly loaned me a linen dress which, she suggested, would add further protection from the sun without being abrasive on my skin. I think she was trying to make up for her heat-on-heat solution. A linen dress? Why not, I thought. When you're on holiday anything goes (except a 4-knot hanky on the head and speedos). At least I could join my friends on the beach, sitting under a large umbrella not only protected me from Mr. Sun and his aggressive heat but shielding me from his obvious wide smirk. It worked, the soft clothing and the large beach umbrella, I was surprised how comfortable I felt.

On the 4th day although my mid-section was sore, I followed the same procedure as the previous day and was happy to sit there in my linen dress, even though I was really disappointed I would not be able to enjoy the marine life that teemed beneath the turquoise colour water of the bay which gently licked the shoreline. Then I had an idea which I thought was nothing short of brilliant; if I lay flat on an airbed placing my snorkel prepared head over the edge, I could float linen dress covered, back to the sun, midriff protected in the sea. I was euphoric at the thought.

I explained my plan to my friends who shared my excitement. Because I was still restricted concerning my arm movement it was decided to place flippers on my feet so I could propel myself in the right direction in the event of the danger of floating out into the open water. I ignored the sniggers as I walked down to the shore clothed with snorkel, goggles, flippers and a linen dress. The embarrassment was worth it compared to the glorious underworld of the ocean I was about to experience. The airbed was carefully placed on the water and while my friends held it steady I gently lay face down in the perfect position. My head firmly supported by the top of the airbed allowed me to gaze into the silent beautiful world below. My feet dangled over the other end of the airbed allowed me to use my webbed flippered feet exactly as I had planned. "What do you think of that Mr. Sun, not smirking now are you thought you had spoilt my holiday, you'll have to rise a little earlier to catch me"?

Feeling absolutely elated both with my nautical view and my victory over my enemy in the sky I forgot about Mr. Sun's partner in crime, Mr. Saltwater. I was already 20 or 30 meters from the shore when the attack came. The saltwater had loosened the blister from around my waist allowing Mr. Ocean's stinging hand to scrape my raw flesh, the pain was paralyzing. I couldn't move. I was afraid to remove my snorkel in case I was unable to manoeuvre my head from the water so my cries for help sounded like a muted foghorn from a ship two miles out at sea.

I panicked. I was drifting further out into the sea and was unable to turn myself around. I finally managed to find some mobility in my right arm and tried to paddle frantically to face in the right direction, I must have done four three-hundred-and-sixty degree turns before I realized I had to use my left flipper to compensate for my flailing right arm. It felt like an eternity. Finally, after breaking through several pain barriers, I reached the seaweed curtained shoreline. It was safe now to gently role into the shallow waters and attempt to stand up and walk free. The manoeuvre was successfully executed, and as I rose up from the shallows the black seaweed clung to me transforming my appearance from a linen dress drag queen into a ferocious bog-monster from the deep. I awkwardly walked up the beach to my friends in a Frankenstein motion scaring the life out of the young children who saw me emerge from the watery abyss. When my friends saw me, I looked at them through my water-speckled goggles (in all the drama, I still hadn't removed the snorkel or the flippers.) My friends were unable to contain themselves at the sight they saw before them laughing, but at the same time realizing I was in pain. They again escorted me back to my hotel room like a group of concerned medics carrying a wounded soldier off the battlefield. What a nightmare, and what a lesson. You cannot do all your sunbathing in one day.

I tell this story to illustrate the simple fact, there are some things in the Christian life that are impossible to realize without submitting to the process; sunbathing is an obvious one, growing in grace is the other. You have to submit to the process; it cannot be achieved in a day.

A young man asked me once what the secret to longevity in the ministry was, and after some serious thought I realized it was, and ever will be, the Grace of God. His Grace to survive the storms of life; His Grace to survive the silence of Heaven; His Grace to survive the sourness of betrayal and rejection, and His Grace to survive the soil. There are so many Christians who live frustrated lives because they fail to apply Grace for the soil. What do I mean when I talk about surviving the soil? I'm simply referring to submitting to the process of growth.

One day, I was reading Jesus' words in John Chapter 12 Verse 27, *'consider the lilies how they grow, they neither toil nor spin, yet I say to you even Solomon in all his glory was not arrayed like one of these'*.

It stopped me in my tracks as I realized Jesus was trying to illustrate one of the most powerful lessons we can learn when it comes to growing healthy as a Christian. He first asks us to *'consider'*. This is not a request for us to give a fleeting thought, but an exaltation to give him our full attention. Consider is a word that refers to the principle of meditation, it means to 'revolve in the mind'. He further reveals to us that in the whole process of Christian growth there is no need to *'toil'* or *'spin'*. The inference is that Christian growth springs from the soil of resting, not working. Grace is the only soil that produces the desired holiness that pleases our father. Nowhere in the New Testament are we exhorted to grow in law. On the contrary, the Grace of God is His only method to transform us into the image of his son, but the one word that captured my attention and to which I applied my 'consideration' was the word *'how'*! 'Consider *how* they grow.' What follows is what the Holy Spirit revealed to me that helped me understand the reason he gives Grace for the Soil.

That one word 'how' forced me to focus not on the end product, the flower, the fruit, but on the process. I was reminded that harvest doesn't just happen. For every flower, fruit, plant or tree, the principle is the same. It begins with a seed then moves through a process of growth 'the how'. Gifts are gifted. Fruit and character are grown. These are principles in Scripture instituted by God that cannot be bypassed. The principle of faithfulness, 'faithful in little, trusted with much'. The principle of servanthood, 'the first shall be last', the principle of radical love 'love your enemies, pray for those who spitefully hurt you'. These principles have been placed into our lives. They are set by God to release potential, reveal motive, test loyalty, and produce a harvest.

One such principle we must understand if things are going to make sense in our lives is seed time and harvest. The *How* of growth. Jesus' words in John Chapter 12 verse 24 are packed with revelation when considering the *How* of the harvest, *'I tell you the truth unless a kernel of wheat is planted in the soil and dies it remains alone, but it's death will produce many new kernels, a plentiful harvest of new lives.'* Of course, we all know with this scripture Jesus is giving us a 'heads up' regarding His death and resurrection, but he is also pulling back the curtain to help us understand the *How* of growth. Imagine I'm holding before you a packet of seeds. Flower seeds. On the front of the package in wonderful technicolour is a photo of the flower the seeds will produce. Alongside that I hold up a potted plant. The reality of the photo. The picture on the packet is now the reality in the pot. My question to you is, how did that happen? How did the picture on the packet become the reality in the pot? It's encouraging to know the picture of what God intends for our lives was already taken before the foundation of the world. What he designed us to be is no surprise to him and God himself submits to his own principle by putting us into time in seed form to go through the process of growth. To experience the *how*.

He did that with Jesus and he does the same with us. The promised Messiah (and worst nightmare for the devil) was described by God in Genesis as a seed (Genesis 3:15). The Father's purpose for Jesus was to be a door. An entrance to heaven for mankind that Adam had closed for all of us because of his disobedience. For thousands of years the Father watched over that seed and faithfully, patiently submitted himself to the process of growth, the *how*. The prophet Isaiah picked up the next part of the process and described the coming Messiah as *'a root out of dry ground'*. Isaiah pictured a rotting stump of earth with one single, tender, green shoot, growing from its dry, seemingly unproductive, nature. But God was at work. Here was a seed growing out of the deadness, out of the dried ground of humanity. God was moving towards His goal, a door. Luke picked up the development of the plant when he declared that *'the child grew and became strong in spirit and increased in stature and favour with God and man'*. No longer a seed or a tender plant, but now a sturdy tree. Jesus grew up in Nazareth to all that knew Him, including his siblings, as just an ordinary tree in God's Garden. No miracles. No special demonstration of power. To the eyes of a watching world just an ordinary tree but to the Father, a door. One day at a baptism ceremony in the River Jordan, that ordinary tree shot head and shoulders above all the other trees God had ever planted as John the Baptist revealed Jesus identity and Heaven shouted its approval. This was no longer a seed or a sapling or a tree, Jesus was now a mighty oak towering above Abraham, Moses, David and Elijah. His branches were thick and heavy with the fruit of healing and blessing and deliverance. Thousands came eat of that fruit and rest in its shade, but God didn't just want a seed or a sapling or a tree or a mighty oak he wanted a door.

Imagine a King who required a special door to the entrance of his home. He commissioned an expert carpenter to search for the right material to make it. Imagine the carpenter and his assistant walking through the forest seeking out that special tree that would produce the right material to make that requested door. As they entered a clearing standing alone, towering above the forest stood a mighty majestic oak tree, centuries old. Quietly growing over the years weathering storms and disease and war. With a glint in his eye the carpenter instructs his assistant to cut it down. The horrified assistant gasps with revulsion at the very thought of putting an axe to its trunk, "you can't do that" the assistant cries out "it's such a waste, it's survived centuries of growth, birds have made their homes in its leafy branches, animals find food and shelter for themselves and families it's just not right". The carpenter turns to his assistant to say, "that may be so, but my employer wants a door, cut it down". In the prime of His life and ministry, Jesus was 'cut off from the land of the living' because the Father didn't want a seed or a sapling or a tree or a mighty oak, He wanted a door. It was all part of The Plan. The purpose of the process was the picture on the packet *'a lamb slain before the foundation of the world,* a door. Judas did not hold the axe that cut the mighty oak, neither was it Pilate, the Chief Priests nor even satan. *'It pleased the Lord to bruise him.'* And, as Jesus submitted to the *'how they grow,'* He was nailed to a cross to fulfil the purpose. When a carpenter places a door on its hinges, he uses a special phrase. He doesn't say I'm going to put this door up; he says I'm going to *hang* this door. When a door is hung it is suspended between the celling and the floor, when Jesus the door was hung, He was suspended between Heaven and earth, for that was the reason for his planting. The Bible says, *'cursed is anyone who is hanged on a tree.'* He hung there, bearing the sins of the whole world; He became a curse for us so we could become the blessed.

Now, finally, God's plan is realized as Jesus rose from the dead. We see the picture on the packet realized, a door. The real purpose of a door is to move from one environment to another, so it is with Jesus, the door. We can move from darkness to light, from sickness to health, from death to life. Jesus said in John chapter 10 *'I am the door'. I came to do my Father's will.* It took centuries of processional growth, but the picture taken before the foundation of the world has now been realized and it all started with a seed. As with Jesus and so with us, the picture of what the Father has prepared us to be, has already been taken. Therefore, it's important we understand and submit to the *'how'* of growth, in order for us to live contented fulfilled lives, knowing that God is perfecting and preparing us constantly as He conforms us to the image of His Son.

There are five principles involved in the law of seed time and harvest, and all are necessary in releasing the potential harvest which God has placed in you. We have to humbly submit to the soil of His grace as He seeks to produce from the seed to the picture on the packet.

In the next chapter we will look at each one. Devotion, Death, Darkness, Dung, and Drainage. Using Scripture coupled with stories from my own journey, my prayer is that whatever stage you're at, the words I write will be inspired by the Holy Spirit to settle your heart and submit to the process.

CHAPTER SIX

GRACE FOR THE SOIL – PART 2

Listening to a TV evangelist one time, not only was I horrified at his manipulative attempts to raise money for his ministry (along with his incredible and unverified claims of miracles performed through his hands), what upset me the most, was his supposed 'revelation from Heaven' that God, in the last days would actually speed up the character-building process in a believer's life. The fruit of the Spirit, he claimed, would be graced in a believer's life bypassing the biblical process for growth. Fruitfulness, he suggested, would be gifted rather than grown. I felt so angry and also very sad for those watching and taking in his words. Those who may be already struggling with all sorts of issues regarding the principle of growing in grace. Nowhere in Scripture does God promise gifted character or gifted fruitfulness. You just cannot bypass the process. There is a 'how they grow' that our hearts need to be established in, I pray what I am about to share with you will release you from the 'toil and spin' of law-based sanctification and the heresy of gifted fruitfulness.

From my observation of fruitfulness as described in Scripture and an understanding drawn from my own personal walk with God for over forty years, I believe we can encapsulate the whole process in 5 simple ways.

Firstly, the Principle of Devotion.

In John, chapter 20, verse 24, Jesus explains. *'Unless a grain of wheat falls into the ground and dies it remains alone'*.

Jesus said if the seed remains alone, isolated, uninvolved and independent, it will remain unproductive. For the potential of the seed to be released it has to become involved and interact with the environment God has designed for that to happen. The one thing that stands between the potential in the seed to the manifestation of the flower is the soil. If you want to return to God empty of the seed and full of fruit, soil is the crucial element. We understand what that means in the natural, but how does that work in the spiritual? What is the soil we need to interact with, get involved with and sow our lives into to release our full potential of fruitfulness? Perhaps these scriptures will give us the answers.

The kingdom of Heaven is like a mustard seed which a man took and sowed in his field. Matthew 13:31

The righteous shall flourish like a palm tree they shall grow like a cedar in Lebanon. Those who are planted in the house of the Lord shall flourish in the courts of our God, they shall bear fruit in old age they shall be fresh and flourishing. Psalm 92:12-14.

There it is – God's field is His house, and the Psalmists declare, those who are planted in it flourish and are fruitful right to the end of their lives. The New Testament verifies this wonderful principle of planting, or what I call, devotion to the soil, not simply placed on its surface but plunged deeply beneath. Not an acquaintance with the soil but a devotion to it.

All the believers (God's seeds) devoted themselves to the apostles teaching, and to the fellowship, and to breaking of bread, and to pray. Acts 2:42.

If we place ourselves on the surface of the local church; surface giving; surface attendants; surface involvement, the winds of preference, relationships or the better option will simply blow you away. It is *our* responsibility to plant ourselves in a local church not just place ourselves. For the seed to release its potential it has to be planted not placed, devoted not acquainted. In Jesus classic parable of the sower and the seed, this danger is prioritized.

As he (the sower) scattered it (the seed) across his field some of the seed fell on the foot path and the birds came and ate it. Mark 4:4.

So many believers place themselves along the footpath of the local church and wonder why they live unproductive and discontented lives. The reason is because only devotion to the soil releases in the seed the fruit it was designed to produce. The human heart is designed to need four things: unconditional love, worship, significance, and community. All four are met through Jesus and His church. Those early Christian seeds demonstrate the reality of those truths in a wonderful way. They devoted themselves to breaking bread for Holy Communion; satisfying their need to know they were unconditionally loved. They devoted themselves to prayer and worship; satisfying their need for transcendence. They devoted themselves to the apostle's doctrine; satisfying their need for significance and they devoted themselves to fellowship; satisfying their need for community.

God's environment to satisfy our hearts and bless the world through our fruitfulness is the soil of the local church. Planted not placed devoted not acquainted. Psalm 92 refers to the material God uses to build His house. Cedars and Palms. Such devotion to the soil of the local church produces the material it needs to build it, Cedars and Palms. Trees of that quality have deep roots and solid foundations because they are devoted to the soil. They are planted. They have taken root and are going nowhere. You know where to find them when needed. God is looking for Cedars and Palms to build his house. Planted, reliable trees when needed. He knows exactly where to find them, planted in the house of the Lord. The amazing thing about a palm tree is that you can cut it but you can't kill it. The nutrients that most trees need to survive are found just under the bark when you cut them, they die. Not so with a Palm tree, its life comes from its core from its heart. Palm-tree-Christians are just like that. They are not surface, shallow, easily offended, or quitters; they have strong hearts. They are planted not placed, devoted not acquainted. *Palm trees bend but they don't break.* Tropical storms can blow most trees off the landscape, not so with Palm trees. They can bend in a storm, sometimes all the way to the ground. When the storm is over, they straighten up and actually become stronger at the place it was bent. A Palm tree is also very sensitive to transplanting. This means Palm trees must be transplanted by an expert. Palm-tree-Christians don't uproot themselves from their place of planting, through offence, hurt, preference, family pressure or boredom, they wait for the expert to transplant them if that is his plan for them. There are many other characteristics of the Palm tree that is worth checking out. God uses nature to teach us practical lessons, especially when it concerns His house, that's why He also uses the analogy of the cedar tree. Planted seed not placed seed. Devoted believers not acquainted believers; these are those God likens to the cedars of Lebanon. Classy trees. They were used for the building of his house in the Old Testament and the same applies in the New Testament. He still needs Cedars of Lebanon to build His Church.

There were four different types of Cedars that Solomon was instructed to harvest in order to build the temple, God's House. The first was the small Cedar. These Cedars were very viscous, in order words, sticky. They dispensed a very sticky sap and as a result were great for transportation. On the journey in order to be used for God's House, the cart they were transported on had to negotiate tricky road turns, and bumps. While other types of trees had to be tied down for safety, the small cedars needed no such restraint. Because of their viscous nature, they stuck together whatever the journey threw at them. God still needs small cedars to build His house. Christians who will stick with the cart however difficult and unpredictable the journey. They don't fall off while negotiating bends, they stick with the vision of the house whatever the crisis and they also encourage other cedars to do the same.

Then we have the Tall Cedar. These majestic trees are so because of their root system. Their roots actually hold the mountain together. God needs tall Cedars to build His House. People whose roots go deep into God's Grace and are devoted to the soil of the local Church. This enables them to hold things together when things seem to be falling apart. They stay when others leave. They encourage when others slander. They stand firm while others falter.

The third type of cedar is the Fire Cedar. These are so-called because they are great firelighters, they easily ignite, great for bringing warmth and excitement. God needs Fire Cedars to build His House. People who are easily ignitable, they don't need constant affirmation or pats on the back. It's in their nature to do what's needed without the need of constant encouragement or title. They just serve. They can't help themselves.

Then lastly, we have the Humming Cedar. These Cedars grow high up on the mountain, and it is said that when a storm rages, and the wind rushes through their branches it sounds like a mass choir. It seems like the whole forest sings. Can you imagine? Humming the tune of praise to God. God needs Humming Cedars to build His house. When others criticize – they sing. They praise. And when others complain about the storm, they, like Paul and Silas, sing through it. That's why it's so important to be planted, devoted to the soil of the local Church. It produces Palms and Cedars, and they can grow no other way.

It's important to realize that God plants seeds not superstars.

Psalm 22:30 says, '*A seed shall serve Him, and it shall be accounted to Him for a generation*'

This verse leads us to the second principle in the process, death.

Jesus' words in John 12:24 explains the principle,

Unless a kernel of wheat is planted in the soil and dies it remains alone, but its death will produce many new kernels a plentiful harvest of new lives.

Once the seed is planted, buried, devoted to the soil, the next part of the process the seed has to endure in order to bear the fruit that potentially lays under its husk is death. It has to die. The Church is not a supermarket where fruit is displayed but a field where fruit is grown. The Church is not the soil designed to glorify yourself but to bury yourself. The soil of the local Church is a wonderful environment to die to self-interest, personal agenda, and sometimes even personal comfort. Before fruitfulness comes death. Dying to selfishness is not a spiritual discipline to develop holiness, but a spiritual dynamic that releases the life of Jesus from within our lives to a lost world. The candle burns bright when the wax submits to its flame, Christ in us burns bright when we die to self. God is looking for seeds that will die, not superstars that can fly.

That verse in Psalm 22 caught my attention and pulsated with revelation regarding the dying seed. Meditating on this verse, it occurred to me that God was looking for an army of believers who were willing to become seeds for this generation. I read a powerful story that brought this truth home to me powerfully. A story of two young men who embodied this truth.

In the 1700's, the Moravians were a persecuted group of believers, particularly so because of their passion for evangelism. The inhumane trade of human trafficking and slavery was rampant across the western world and the Moravians were not merely horrified at what was taking place, they wanted to do something to reach those poor people with the Gospel. Two young men came forward with a plan of action which involved incredible sacrifice. They offered to sell themselves into slavery. So in the early 1700's a ship left Copenhagen with two young men on board; John Dober, a carpenter and David Neichman, a potter. As they stood on the deck of the departing ship, they waved goodbye to their friends and their family shouting these words *'May the Lamb that was slain receive a harvest with our sacrifice'*. This was a picture not of two superstars being sent but two seeds being sown. Historians tell us that as a result of these two seeds dying in the soil, a whole generation of slaves found Christ.

I have the privilege of preaching to thousands of people across the globe and I believe part of the reason that I am doing what I'm doing is because a man I once knew named Stephen was prepared to become a seed. As I mentioned at the beginning, I was raised on a housing estate in a small Welsh village called *Resolven*. Entertainment was hard to come by, so we had to amuse ourselves as children. We particularly looked forward to the weekly Baptist Church open air service in our street. We loved it. Not because of the content, but because of the opportunity to abuse. They sang, we laughed. They preached, we mocked. And we especially mocked Stephen. Stephen was our age and there he stood, blowing his trumpet, red faced but man, he was bold! To be honest, he couldn't play very well. If we were near an ocean his playing would probably attract a pod of whales! But, play he did, under a barrage of abuse from his peers. One Saturday something strange started to happen in my heart. As my mouth was shouting the ridicule, my heart began to feel respect for Stephen. Here was a young boy, my age, prepared to stand up in the middle of the street in front of his kids his own age, to receive gut wrenching verbal attacks and all because he truly believed in what he was doing. He was proud of the God he stood for.

What took place in that moment that had such a profound effect upon my life was that a seed was dying. Stephen himself was prepared to become a seed and as a result, he touched my life in such a way that it would be a nudge, directing me to the cross where I too would be prepared to lay down my life and follow Jesus. You may not be incredibly talented or gifted or privileged in many ways; you may look at your life and think how can I impact my world, my place of work, my school, my university and my family? You can emulate Stephen – offer yourself as a seed to God. You will be amazed at what will burst forth and bless your world. So then, before the seed can produce and release the potential within its shell, it has to be devoted. It has to experience death and then has to endure darkness. The darkness of obscurity.

See how the farmer waits for the precious fruit of the earth. Waiting patiently for it. James 5:7

The Master Gardener knows when it's time for you to be seen. Part of you has to be lost before you burst out of the ground. The shell around the seed is not the life ordained for you. That shell must interact with the right elements that would bring death to it. We must endure the darkness of obscurity, out of sight, unnoticed and sometimes overlooked, we have to stay there long enough for the process to do its work. To split the outer shell and release the potential within. So many talented, able, gifted people feel they are ready to be seen, ready to step into what they know to be their destiny, but they lack the patience to stay in the dark and trust the timing of God.

Moses learned the hard way. He knew he was the one to deliver the Hebrews from their bondage *'It came into his heart'*, to do something about their salvation. He definitely had a burden, it was a legitimate passion, he was God's choice; but the missing element was timing and ultimately, the timing of our release into whatever God has for us is in His hands. Moses endured forty years in the darkness of obscurity; forty years believing he had failed and no longer of any use to God, but when the master gardener said, *'now is the time for harvest'*, Moses returned to Egypt with more than a burden. He returned with a *call*. A burden can be a call in gestation. A burden will take you so far; but a call will take you all the way. A burden runs when confronted with a Pharaoh because it's self-perpetuated, it's underdeveloped fruit. It's an impatient seed hating the darkness. A call is a seed that has endured the darkness. A call is fruit in God's timing. A call has nowhere else to go. It has no exit plan. It knows its time of release has come and is intimidated by no one and nothing. With a burden, Moses killed one Egyptian and buried him in the sand. After forty years in darkness, he returned with a call and saw God destroy a whole army and bury them in the sea. Be patient, allow the darkness of the soil to do its work.

A study of the Apostle Paul's life would be profitable to marinate your heart with this principle. At conversion, Saul died, and Paul was planted, devoted into the local Church (Acts 9:19-20, 26-28). For the next fourteen years he endured the darkness of obscurity in his hometown of Tarsus. As amazing as he was regarding his testimony and gifting, the Church grew without his input, (Acts 9:29-31). When the time was right, God sent Barnabas to bring him to Antioch where after some further fine-tuning, he was released into his calling, (Acts 13:1-2).

We must learn, and often we do the hard way, that we are not indispensable and when God wants to release us into something which He has prepared for us, He knows exactly where to find us. From the very first day of my own conversion, I knew, deep down, working a nine to five job was not how I wanted to spend the rest of my life. I just knew God had called me to serve him in a full-time capacity, preaching and singing. But it took a further ten years for that dream to be realized. During that time, I had to learn many pride-demolishing lessons about God's principles regarding preparation and timing, much of which I wrote in my book *Prepared for Greatness (Reyla ministries, 2004)*. One of those lessons that God had to teach me was the necessity of enduring the darkness of the soil. My conversion caused quite a stir in my locality because for most of my teenage years, I was a member of a high-profile pop group named *'Robbie & Ray & the Jaguars'*. And as I may have already mentioned, we were one of the first local bands to be signed by 'Decca Records' the recording company that famously rejected the Beatles. (But signed us!) As a result of my local fame, after my conversion, I became a celebrity in another environment – my local Church. *The Peniel Pentecostal Church, Glynneath*, South Wales. *Glynneath* then had a population of about seven-thousand, and the Church, after I became a member was about 60 people. Sunday Salvations were pretty rare so when I became part of that congregation you can imagine the attention I received. I went from being celebrated in the entertainment world to being celebrated in the Church world, and I loved it! I loved the attention and the opportunity to share my testimony many times during that first year following Jesus. But then something began to happen, my popularity began to wane. Other people were being asked to take part in the Sunday services and I was being overlooked. Along with a now mundane lifestyle, with a job working in a paint store, my sense of value and importance was taking a beating.

My youth leader at that time saw what was happening and graciously took me aside and taught me a lesson that changed my perspective regarding serving Jesus. He began to explain, in detail, a program he saw on television the previous evening. It was a program recording in detail an actual open-heart surgery procedure. He went into every gory aspect explaining the instruments the surgeon used, being careful to remind me that when the surgeon finished using one instrument, he laid it on the table then picked up another instrument. While trying to figure out why he thought I would be interested in open heart surgery he stopped, looked purposefully into my face and said 'You see, Ray, when the surgeon finished using one instrument and then placed it on the table, that instrument never lost its value or importance just because it wasn't in his hand.' He then drove the lesson home 'Ray, whether you're in God's hand being used and seen, or on the table, seemingly overlooked and discarded, it makes no difference, because your value is not connected to your profile but your relationship. To God you are just as valuable whether you are in his hand or on the table. Learn to be content with either.'

It hurt a little, I felt a little humiliated, but it was one of the best lessons I could learn so early on in my Christian life. Your value and effectiveness in God's kingdom are not dependent on your exposure, profile or activity. It's how you patiently and contentedly relate it to how you handle the obscurity, while others are being exalted. It's amazing to think after all the spectacular events surrounding the Virgin Birth, Mary lived a seemingly mundane life in Nazareth for thirty years until she saw the reason for it all. Very often, the real miracle is in the mundane. It's not about what God is doing *through* you; it's about what God is doing *in* you.

So, devotion, death, darkness and as we all know no plant can grow strong and healthy without dung! The fourth element of the 'how' factor.

Fertilizer is essential in producing good fruit. Someone once said what the devil designed to cause a stink in your life, God will use as fertilizer for new growth. That's where trials and testing fit into the positive area of our Christian growth. God uses them as dung; that is, fertilizer to produce strong, sturdy plants.

In Philippians 3:7-8 KJV Paul said, *'The loss of all things...'* Whatever that was, did not depress him as a negative but fired him up as he realized that even rejection, loss and betrayal was used as dung by God to deepen his relationship with Jesus. The body of Christ needs to know the message of the dying seed and realize when the outer crust of the seed is burst open, it actually becomes fertilizer for the new life coming forth. Although persecution and trials are no fun, God encourages us to see how he uses what seems to be a negative and turns it into a positive.

> *Now no chastening seems to be joyful for the present, but painful; nevertheless, afterward it yields the peaceable fruit of righteousness to those who have been trained by it.*
> Hebrews 12:11 (NKJV)

Finally, no growth would be possible for any plant without regular drainage. There needs to be a constant flow of water. For us the analogy is the same. Our healthy growth in God is dependent on a constant flow of His Word of Grace; Heaven's drainage system designed to produce the picture on the packet. The water of the Word needs to be channelled through our lives because without that consistent drainage, the fruit desired would be non-existent. For years the Church has produced inedible fruit and stunted growth because of 'poor drainage'. She has been fed law-based water instead of grace-based water. The result? A harvest of self-righteous, performance based, judgmental Pharisees. The only drainage provided by God to produce good fruit is Grace. Nowhere in the New Testament does God encourage us to grow in law. The biggest need for the Church right now is life-giving drainage. There has been a drought in the body of Christ for years. The garden is insipid and dry, Christian fruitfulness is weak and distasteful. The reason? Bad drainage. It has not been watered by the grace of God.

But I hear a sound of an abundance of rain. Torrents of grace, filling ditches and irrigating furrows flowing into local Churches, which were once barren wastelands, and are now seeing fresh green foliage and luscious fruit grow. Our Christian roots are bursting with the life-producing fruit-enriching water of the grace of God. Sadly, in many parts of the world, the Church has been irrigated with stones instead of bread. Snakes instead of fish and scorpions instead of eggs.

In Matthew 7:9-10 NLT Jesus says,

"You parents – if your children ask for a loaf of bread, do you give them a stone instead? Or if they ask for a fish, do you give them a snake? Of course not!

For years, God's people have been stoned from the pulpit. Instead of the bread of grace, the manna from Heaven, they've been beaten and bruised by stones of law and judgement. Instead of an irrigated garden bursting with colour and vitality, we see a garden vandalized by legalism and law. For years, the Church has been poisoned by snake venom instead of sustained by fish. Fish is one of the healthiest foods one can eat. Law-based preaching is so criminal; not only will it rob you of healthy food but fill your heart with the venom of the Pharisees.

In Luke 11:11-12 (NLT), Jesus refers to another type of food on the menu that should never be ordered. Scorpion soup. It's replaced the original entry placed there by the chef – eggs, any way you want them! The scorpion is subtle because its sting is in its tail. Law-based preaching is the same, there's a sting in its tail. Fill in the blanks, 'God loves you, but…, You're saved, but…, God has forgiven you your past sins, but…. Scorpion based preaching has a sting in its butt!

Our Father does not feed us with scorpions but eggs and serves them up any way you want them; boiled, poached, omelettes, fried. The word of Grace irrigates every area of our lives. Paul's final words to the Ephesian elders sums it up for me as I close this chapter.

"And now I entrust you to God and the message of his grace that is able to build you up and give you an inheritance with all those he has set apart for himself. Acts 20:32 NLT, 32

CHAPTER SEVEN

GRACE FOR SADNESS

I thank God that Jesus was fully human as well as fully God. The Bible says he was *'touched with the feelings of our infirmities'*. He *'carried our sorrows and was acquainted with our grief' (Isa 53)*. Jesus knew what is was like to go around doing good, feeling bad. He met the needs of around twenty-thousand hungry people while grieving the loss of his cousin. He wept with great sadness over a people He loved, but who rejected him in return. He chose to forgive those who organized His execution, while enduring the most intense emotional trauma. He chose to wash the feet of his betrayer, even though the pain of betrayal was ripping through his heart. Jesus knew what it was like to experience sadness on many levels, so He is well able not only to empathize, but to send in reinforcements in the form of 'Grace Alone'. For some of you reading these words, the sadness you're experiencing could be the result of a relational breakdown, a dream that has died, a sudden tragic event or something so devastating words have lost their ability to describe the pain. I pray this chapter will help you apply God's only remedy for your broken heart, His Grace Alone.

The words of David captured in Psalm 143, describes the characteristics of sadness in a way we can all relate to. That's what I love about the Psalms written by David, he holds nothing back, he's totally unrestrained in his emotional outbursts to God and in so doing lets us into a world we are all familiar with. The words you are about to read were written during a great season of sadness for David. The heady days of adoration as a giant killer were long gone. The taste of the kingly anointing oil was a distant memory or perhaps it never happened at all. Perhaps the whole event of being chosen king, was just a figment of what he thought was an arrogant imagination. Here, in Psalm 143, years of rejection, persecution and constant harassment from King Saul, he finds himself hiding in a cave with three-hundred losers trying to make sense of it all.

Is that where you are? Trying to make sense of it all as you retrace the sequence of events in your mind, desperately trying to find the key where it all turned bad. Perhaps that same key can be used to rectify the whole mess. Sadness rolls into our lives like the waves on a beach and with each wave, the debris of the past, 'could haves and should haves' wash across the sandy beaches of your heart. You pick up the trash only to find another wave brings in more inconsolable pain. Let's read about David's sadness, described in the first six verses of Psalm 143 and discover that in the midst of his brokenness, he offers us hope on how to walk through the sad times of life.

> *For the enemy hath persecuted my soul; he hath smitten my life down to the ground; he hath made me to dwell in darkness, as those that have been long dead. herefore is my spirit overwhelmed within me; my heart within me is desolate. I remember the days of old; I meditate on all thy works; I muse on the work of thy hands. I stretch forth my hands unto thee: my soul thirsteth after thee, as a thirsty land. Selah.* Psalm 143:3-6 (KJV)

Once, when I read these verses, I was going through my own season of sadness and didn't know how to pray. David came to my rescue and not only gave understanding to the texture of sadness but how to express it to God even though it made no sense to him. *'An enemy has persecuted my soul, he has smitten my life to the ground, my spirit is overwhelmed within me and my heart within me is desolate'.* Wow! Does that describe how you feel right now?

When I read those words, this is how I interpreted them through my own experience. 'God, my mind and emotions are under constant attack from the enemy. Things are falling apart; this sadness is dominating my life and there seems to be no visible evidence of improvement. And the worst thing about the season of sadness is the darkness.' *'He makes me dwell in darkness,'* Lord, I can deal with the abuse, the unfair treatment, but what I can't handle is the darkness.' Probably the worst thing about the seasons of darkness, is the sadness. You can't see a way out, a way through, but hang in there, because here in the darkness, what you are experiencing right now, can be used by God, not only to perfect you, but to bless others. From your perspective, the darkness is preventing the purposes of God being worked out, when in fact, the opposite is true. From your perspective, the darkness is obliterating God's gaze into our predicament but according to Psalm 139 11-12, not even the thickest darkness can hide our situation from God.

> *I could ask the darkness to hide me and the light around me to become night – 12 but even in darkness I cannot hide from you. To you the night shines as bright as day. Darkness and light are the same to you.* Psalm 139:11-12 (NLT)

To really understand how to walk through the dark times of life, we have to draw encouragement from our Saviour Jesus. The darkness He experienced and endured on Calvary's hill, two thousand years ago, can shed light into the confusion of blackness.

> *Now from the sixth hour until the ninth hour there was darkness over all the land. And about the ninth hour Jesus cried out with a loud voice, saying, "Eli, Eli, lama sabachthani?" that is, "My God, My God, why have You forsaken Me?"* Matthew 27:45-46 (NKJV)

It's comforting to know that Jesus understands the trauma of darkness because He's already been there. While experiencing my own personal season of 'I don't know'; craving answers while enduring *'the unplanned places of destiny'*, Jesus whispered to my heart, *'Ray, it's enough for you to know that I know'*. His message to us from the darkness of Calvary's cross, as we endure seasons of gloom is, *'I know'*. While meditating on these verses, I began to realize that darkness, although undesirable, emotionally can be used by God to perfect us in a way that nothing else can. There are four things regarding the darkness Jesus experienced that can give us great insight into why sometimes God allows us to experience it. Firstly, the darkness was comprehensive. It covered 'all the land', when you encounter seasons of darkness, it affects every area of your life – spirit, soul and body. It covers the whole land. But thank God, it doesn't last forever. Thank God, we pass through it, not set up camp there. The Bible says, the darkness Jesus endured, lasted from the sixth to the ninth hour, but it was Jesus' response to the darkness that caught my attention. *'He cried out in a loud voice, my God, my God, why?'*. Never had Jesus prayed *so* loud, and never was Heaven *more* silent. It's one thing to experience dark times knowing the reason why, it's another thing to walk through dark times not only bewildered as to the reason why, but also to begin to believe that God is not in it with you.

When Jesus was enduring a season of God forsakenness, crying out for help from His Father, what hurt Him even more than the searing pain running havoc through his body, was the heart-breaking hopelessness that resulted from a silent Heaven. I began to learn something about Heaven's seeming lack of response that helped me so much to endure my seasons of darkness and it is this, *'Heaven may be silent, but it's never deaf'*. The writer to the Hebrews, while describing Jesus passionate cry from the cross, gives us incredible insight into that thought.

...who, in the days of His flesh, when He had offered up prayers and supplications, with vehement cries and tears to Him who was able to save Him from death and was heard because of His godly fear. Hebrews 5:7 (NKJV)

'And (he) was heard'. (Parenthesis added)

There's nothing worse than crying for help knowing no one is listening, no one can hear you; but be encouraged, that's never the case with your relationship with God. You may not understand His nonresponse, but rest assured, your cry has been heard. He knows and He is using even the darkness to perfect something in you so that you can be a source of blessing to someone else. The amazing thing about God's grace is that even through the sadness of dark times. God uses the pain and rejection and a silent Heaven as material to display His strength and produce in us a level of trust and patience into a life source for others.

Hebrews 5:7-9 in the Amplified Bible tells us,

In the days of His earthly life, Jesus offered up both [specific] petitions and [urgent] supplications [for that which He needed] with fervent crying and tears to the One who was [always] able to save Him from death, and He was heard because of His reverent submission toward God [His sinlessness and His unfailing determination to do the Father's will]. Although He was a Son [who had never been disobedient to the Father], He learned [active, special] obedience through what He suffered. And having been made perfect [uniquely equipped and prepared as Saviour and retaining His integrity amid opposition], He became the source of eternal salvation [an eternal inheritance] to all those who obey Him

Everyone God uses as a life source were perfected during the dark times of life; Abraham endured fourteen years under a silent Heaven waiting for God's promise that through Him, all the nations of the earth would be blessed; Joseph was used as a life source to save his family and a nation.

But don't be upset, and don't be angry with yourselves for selling me to this place. It was God who sent me here ahead of you to preserve your lives. Genesis 45:5, (NLT)

Joseph became a life source of blessing to millions, but it was during the seventeen years of darkness that God perfected him. When it must have felt like Heaven was totally disinterested in his pain, Heaven was actually preparing Joseph using the material of betrayal, rejection, humiliation, sadness, and a silent Heaven to perfect him as a life source. Another classic example, of course, is Moses. For forty years living as a fugitive in the backside of the Midian desert riddled with shame, the guilt he must have lived with, having to run for his life, the life of a coward in the face of the wrath of Pharaoh. Forty years of living with the sadness of shame, forty years of living under a silent Heaven. Then, in one brief encounter with the God he thought had forgotten him, all was made clear. It was all designed by Heaven to prepare and perfect Moses as a life source for his shackled people. He had made such a mess of things, he believed he would never hear that voice again. Forty years of darkness, forty years of living with the sadness of a failed mission, but all the while, although Heaven was silent, it certainly wasn't deaf. All was revealed to Moses during that life changing conversation high up on a rugged mountain, through a burning bush, in one brief moment those forty years of asking why was answered.

> *Then the Lord told him, "I have certainly seen the oppression of my people in Egypt. I have heard their cries of distress because of their harsh slave drivers. Yes, I am aware of their suffering. So I have come down to rescue them from the power of the Egyptians and lead them out of Egypt into their own fertile and spacious land. It is a land flowing with milk and honey – the land where the Canaanites, Hittites, Amorites, Perizzites, Hivites, and Jebusites now live. Look! The cry of the people of Israel has reached me, and I have seen how harshly the Egyptians abuse them. Now go, for I am sending you to Pharaoh. You must lead my people Israel out of Egypt."* Exodus 3:7-10 New Living Translation

Essentially, God was saying to Moses that day, 'I've been listening for many years Moses, I have been fully aware of the suffering of my people, but I needed to perfect a life source to lead them out and that life source is you. All that sadness and silence and shame was actually the material I needed for my Grace to build you, shape you and perfect you for the destiny I pre-destined for you.'.

I don't know what has blocked out the sun shining for you, but one thing I know for sure, the darkness will pass, Heaven will speak and, once made perfect, you too will become a life source for many. One of the hardest things I have found as I have sought to work out my calling as a minister is how to negotiate a silent Heaven, a sad heart and a dark place and to do it with a contented attitude. Paul the Apostle said, *'For I have learned, in whatever state I am, to be content'*. How do we do that? How do we consistently minister effectively or live as a Christian effectively when our heart is continually bombarded with darkness, disappointment and discouragement. David comes to our help with a very simple answer *'I stretch forth my hands unto thee'*.

Picture David, as he stood in the darkness of Adullum's cave, still tasting the anointing oil that was poured over him seventeen years earlier. The promise of kingship now a distant memory. Since that momentous day when he was called in from the fields to be anointed as Israel's king by the prophet Samuel, things had gone from bad to worse. He'd been driven from his family, his place of worship and worst of all, his sense of destiny. Yet, in the darkness of that cave, which in reality reflected the darkness in his heart, he stretched forth his hands to God. That simple gesture is loaded with a profound spiritual lesson that will equip us to negotiate any dark season with a contented heart. When I was a child, we played a game called *Blind Man's Bluff*. First, your eyes were blindfolded, next you were spun around and had to walk like a mummy with arms outstretched trying to find your friends who you knew were in the room, but you could not locate. As you walk with outstretched arms, what you communicated to your friends on a nonverbal level was 'I can't see you, I can't feel you, but I know you are there somewhere'. That was David's secret to walk through a dark time keeping his heart free from spiritual disease that could disqualify him from being the life source God was perfecting him to be.

In that dark time, David simply turned to God. Again, this may sound simplistic but when life does not make sense, the devil can tempt us to turn anywhere but to God. We can turn bitter, we can turn angry, we can turn back, or we can turn away. When self-pity seems a better option, when giving up seems the only road to take, when the pain of a broken heart would be a legitimate reason to seek revenge, that's the time to stretch forth your hands to God. Not doing so, disqualifies us from being a life source to others because the 'issues of life' have become contaminated. As a photograph is developed in a dark room, to be a blessing to others, so God uses the dark times of our lives to develop qualities in us that will later prove to be a life source for many. Turning to God in dark times, keeps you in a position to minister to others.

GRACE FOR SEASONS

I remember having the awesome, although intimidating, experience of preaching in a conference with the amazing T.D. Jakes. It was in South Africa at Rhema Church, pastored at that time, by Ray Macauley. Intimidating, because my session was *after* his. How does anyone follow T.D Jakes? During his message on Romans chapter eight, he said something that truly had a profound effect on my life. He said, 'At the beginning of Romans 8, Paul said *"I know that the whole of creation groans for the revealing of the Son of God."* At the end of Romans 8 he says, *"For I know that all things work together for good…"* but in the middle of Romans 8 he says, *"I don't know…"*. He went on to say that very often at the beginning of a season, a prospect, a dream, we are all excited, full of faith, and we just know this is going to be successful. At the end of a season, when our dream has been through the wringer, we can see how God used the good, bad and the ugly to eventually make it all work together for good.

But, it's in the middle, just like in Romans 8, it's in the middle that Paul said, '*I don't know*'. That's when trust is really developed – when we go through seasons of '*I don't know*'. As he illustrated from his own life how he negotiated those '*I don't know*' seasons, T D Jakes told us that he started to pray the '*I don't know*' prayer. It went something like this;

> *'Don't give me anything I can't handle because I don't know when to say no; open the doors I need to walk through and close the doors I don't need to walk through because I don't know which is which. Take the people out of my life I don't need for this season and bring the people into my life that I do need, because I can't distinguish a Judas from a John. Help me understand and negotiate the seasons of my life, because I just don't know.'*

I started to pray that prayer and, believe me, it worked! As I mentioned earlier, negotiating the seasonal changes in our lives can be scary, and even more so when we don't know why. That must have been the experience of the women who turned up at Jesus' tomb on Resurrection Morning. They arrived at the tomb to anoint a dead body, not a resurrected one. They had made the decision to spend time around the dead body of Jesus. Their motives were good, their preparation was thorough, mentally and sacrificially, to spend time in a cemetery not a resurrection party. The season was about to change, God had a powerful lesson to teach them and through them, us.

The words from the angels must have sounded so insensitive to their grieving hearts and those words may seem so insensitive to your situation, but God is about to grace you for a change of season. *'Why do you seek the living amongst the dead? He is not here...'*

In fact, the angel was saying, 'you won't find answers here, because you won't find your answers in dead places. As you read these words, some of you are in your *'I don't know'* season because, like those women in the cemetery, God is saying to you 'why do you seek the living in the dead areas of your life?'

Seasons; mentalities; dreams; lifestyles; thoughts; habits; methods that are long dead; but still you return to put flowers on their graves. Still, you hang around something that has died, hoping to find life. The longer you hang around this cemetery; the more ineffective you become on reaching this world with the message of hope. The more stuck you become in a season that's dead. The grace He gave you for that season will be the same grace that will sustain you in the next season. But, for that to happen, you must leave the cemetery.

I remember watching a very moving documentary on the life of Kodiak Bears, from Alaska, particularly focusing on a mother and her cub. In one scene, the mother bear was reaching under the crevice of a rock to retrieve some honey from a bee's nest, suddenly and without warning, to the horror of the film crew, there was a rockslide, instantly killing the mother. It was so moving to see the little cub hang around the dead body of its mother, whining and touchingly hoping for signs of life. Of course, the film crew were under strict instructions to not interfere with the natural life of any animal they were filming, and finally after five days of hanging around his mother's corpse, the need to survive was greater than the need to grieve. It took a realization that his mother was dead to force him to find life elsewhere. There had to be a revelation of death before there came a passion for life. The same applies to us. There are many reading these words right now that need to leave the cemetery. You need to walk away from dead dreams. Dreams you placed all your hope in only to see them die.

I think of King David and the whole tragic scenario played out with Bathsheba. Bathsheba's husband was murdered on the orders of David.

Bathsheba was pregnant; David had been found out. God had spared his life and kingship, but the baby born was now fighting for his life. All of David's dreams regarding succession were wrapped up in that child. David wept, fasted and pleaded with God to let the child live. David did everything within his power to keep that dream alive, but it was not to be. When the realization of the child's death hit him, David gives an example to us on how to walk away from a dead dream. 2 Samuel 12:20 (NLT) says

> *Then David got up from the ground, washed himself, put on lotions,[a] and changed his clothes. He went to the Tabernacle and worshiped the Lord. After that, he returned to the palace and was served food and ate.*

As painful as it is to walk away from the graveside of a dead dream, it has to be done for a new dream to be birthed. A new dream was about to be born; Solomon. Before that could happen, David had to leave the cemetery of a dream that died. I firmly believe God can resurrect dreams, but very often He allows one to die in order for another to be birthed. What dream has died in your life? Perhaps you were responsible for the death of that dream, perhaps it was the result of unforeseen circumstances or evil-minded people. Whatever the cause, it's time to stop asking why and walk away. It's time to stop laying flowers on the grave of that dead dream. There is no life coming from it. A new dream is waiting to be conceived, perhaps God, through this book is saying to you, '*Why do you seek the living amongst the dead?*' There is a Solomon waiting to be born, but he cannot be birthed until you leave the cemetery of a dead dream.

Some of you need to walk away from dead relationships. The story of Lot and the judgment of Sodom and Gomorrah, is probably one of the most universally known stories in the bible, reading it one day, while thinking about dead relationships, God began to show me some very helpful practical steps on how to walk away from the cemetery of dead relationships. You can get an overview of the plot by reading Genesis 19:14-26. Lot, his wife and his children had lived in those evil cities for some time. A place they should never have chosen to live, with relationships they should have never built. As far as God was concerned, Sodom and Gomorrah were finished. He had to get out and get his family out. While reading the whole narrative, two statements struck me that have great relevance to the subject at hand. The angel, under instruction from God to rescues Lot from the impending judgment, urged Lot to "*hurry, I can do nothing while you are here*" (Verse 22 pp).

The angel could do nothing with Lot's future, until he was out of that dead place. Relationships can be the greatest source of joy and heartache. They also can be the greatest hindrance to the fulfilling of a dream. The people who stand with you are not necessarily the ones that finish with you. Not all those people who are with you right now, are helpful to you stepping out of the boat. It's important to have the right kind of people in your life that fuel encouragement and positivity.

I think of Peter about to step over the side of the boat, about to attempt something no one had ever done before. I wonder what advice and encouragement he had from the group in the boat. I wonder if Peter talked to them first and asked, 'what do you think I should do?' Letting my imagination run wild and picturing myself about to ask advice from people who weren't prepared to do what I was about to do I'm reminded of some things: firstly, don't ask advice from people who don't want to step out of the boat. Don't ask advice from people who've done nothing, asked nothing, failed but kept trying. Perhaps their advice would sound something like this, 'Hey Peter, before you attempt this crazy thing, have you considered the percentages? Have you checked the stats on how many others have succeeded at what you're attempting to do? How many people have walked on water apart from Jesus? The odds are against you Peter!' Of course, it's wise to consider the counsel of people, but make sure those people are rooting for your success, that trust and support your decisions, even though they don't understand and will be the type of people who won't say 'I told you so' if it doesn't work out.

When I planted the King's Church in Newport, Wales in 1989, I had many who presented me with the statistics, in particular, my lack of experience. I was reminded of my lack of college education and my lack of experience in church planting, but I know I had heard from God. I presented my 'advisors' stats to the Lord for His scrutiny and He said to me, *'Your lack of experience will work to your advantage, because, like Peter, you will have to focus on Me and listen to My instruction.'* He also pointed out the fact that Noah was not often seen for his boatbuilding experience. He was asked to build something he'd never seen before. Noah's success was in his lack of experience, because he had to rely solely on God's instructions concerning the shape and size. I'm so glad I didn't listen to the statisticians, otherwise there wouldn't be a church in Newport today, the means whereby multiple thousands have been helped spiritually and socially. Thus, possibly, the guys in the boat could have directed Peter's attention to the problem. 'Hey Peter, you can't just attempt to walk on water! Have you not noticed there's a storm raging?

At least wait until the storm subsides.' Compassionate advice, but when God gives you a *Rhema* word, "Come", it matters not. When God gives you a word to get out of the boat, it does not even consider the problem. Perhaps they could have reminded Peter of his tendency to be unstable; 'Take your personality into consideration, Peter, before you take a step, you know what you're like. Remember when Jesus called you three names in five minutes. Jesus Himself said you're unstable; He called you Simon, Satan and rock in the same breath; is this just another one of those impetuous decisions that will just get you into more trouble? And, what about your past? You haven't exactly been a model of preparation, have you? Your bad decisions and unwillingness to listen to advice has caused you disaster after disaster.' Perhaps they were on a roll now, entrenched in their negativity, observing Peter's 'second-guess' expression, believing their rationale was getting through. They could have questioned the point of it all. 'Why risk your life to walk on the water? What's the point? What have you got to prove? What good is it going to do anyone? Come on, Peter, let's be practical about this.'

But you have heard from God, like Peter, like Lot, it's personal and God can do nothing more with your destiny until you're away from those dead relationships. It could be a business relationship; romantic relationship; an unproductive Christian relationship, it doesn't matter how attached you are to them. Lot's wife examples to us just what happens when we nostalgically hanker after relationships that have had their season.

> But Lot's wife, behind him, **looked back**, and she became a pillar of salt. Genesis 19:26 (emphasis added)

She was frozen in time. Some of you may have left the relationship, but still mourn the loss of it. You are still looking back with emotional eyes, not Kingdom eyes and it's freezing you in time. You can't go back; you can't move forward. You're stuck in time. It's time to walk away from sentimentality toward memories and walk away from the coveting of dead relationships. Some of you need to walk away from dead seasons. When seasons change, so does God's way of doing things. The problem is, we want Him to operate in the same way, use the same methods of procedure in His dealings with us as in previous seasons. We just don't like change. Because of our reticence to move into a new season, we tend to sometimes canonise traditions formed, and immortalise people used by God. A young twenty-five-year-old king in the Old Testament examples for us just how we are to deal with this problem in 2 Kings 18:1-4.

> *In the third year of Hoshea son of Elah, king of Israel, Hezekiah*
> *the son of Ahaz, king of Judah, began to reign. He was twenty-*
> *five years old when he began to reign, and he reigned twenty-*
> *nine years in Jerusalem. His mother's name was Abi the daughter*
> *of Zechariah. And he did what was right in the eyes of the LORD,*
> *according to all that David his father had done. He removed the*
> *high places and broke the pillars and cut down the Asherah. And*
> *he broke in pieces the bronze serpent that Moses had made, for*
> *until those days the people of Israel had made offerings to it*
> *(it was called Nehushtan).*

For hundreds of years, Israel had worshipped and sanctified a method God had used once. When serpents were running rampant in the Israeli camp during the forty years in the wilderness, God instructed Moses to hold a brass serpent, strap it to a pole and lift it up high. His instruction was that if anyone who had been bitten, just looked at the serpent on the pole, they would be healed. Obviously, this was a wonderful picture of what God was going to do through His Son on the cross hundreds of years later. But, because of this incredible miracle, the people sanctified the symbol and still looked upon it years later expecting the same results.

There is an innate romanticism in all of us that wants to raise its head when the challenges of the present and future loom before us. It's no wonder that many denominations and churches speak more of days past, when it all began for them, rather than the present and the future season into which they are entering. It's imperative we don't sanctify methods used by God in seasons past. Thank God for them, yes, but let's be open to the new things He is about to do. God doesn't clone His methods, if that was the case, Peter would have started 'Shadow Ministries' and 'Water-Walking Ministries'. Paul would have perfected 'Handkerchief Ministries' and Samson; 'Jawbone Ministries'!

I believe passionately in refusing to sanctify God's method of doing things, because, for a while, it seriously hindered my ministry reaching young people in schools during the Nineteen-Eighties. My denomination had used certain methods of presenting the gospel in schools and at that time it was the only model I had to work from. Every day I would come away from a day's ministry in a school frustrated and embarrassed because the method just wasn't working. Maybe thirty years previous it had proved very effective, but for me it was like David trying to take Goliath out wearing Saul's armour. For six years in the nineteen sixties I was a rock singer and entertainer. Singing and humour were my slingshot.

I was comfortable with that sort of weaponry. It was a proven method of keeping people entertained and interested. I felt God say to me, *'I'm not going to anoint who you want to be, or who others want you to be'*. So, with respect, I refused to wear Saul's armour anymore and began to use my own method of killing giants. I started to introduce music and humour as a means to communicate the gospel in schools and the effect was remarkable. Hundreds of young people found Christ because I refused to sanctify a method that may have been successful in one season, but not in another. So radical was my method of reaching young people to my denomination, when training their school workers, the church used me as an example of how *not* to do it!

I heard of a church in the USA, that hired a Pastoral expert to help them find out why their church, a once nine thousand strong congregation, had dwindled to just one hundred people and many of them were beyond retirement age. He quickly discovered, while they wanted things to change, they themselves did not want to change. Decades ago, those same people had successfully practiced mission and brought the gospel into their culture in a relevant way. But, as times changed, they did not. They preferred to wallow in the nostalgia of a season gone than grasp the opportunity of the present. Ecclesiastes 7:10 hits it on the head:

> *Do not say, "Why were the old days better than these?" For it is not wise to ask such questions.*

Pastor Hollick was asked to Pastor a church in Glossop, England, it had been one of the fastest growing Pentecostal churches in the United Kingdom in its early days. It was founded by John Houghton in 1888 who was a Pentecostal revolutionary in his generation. The sad thing was, every succeeding generation right up to 1982 had stayed, nostalgically, in the 1800's. They refused to redecorate the church, and the bible lay open on Jeremiah 29; Houghton's favourite passage of scripture. Not one page had been turned in one hundred years. In order to follow Hezekiah's example, Hollick cancelled church meetings for a week, took a chain saw and demolished the pews and pulpit and brought the church into the 1980's! Sunday morning came, and eighty-year-old Edith nearly left because she thought she had come to the wrong church! The church began to grow because someone had the guts to demolish the serpent on the pole.

Nostalgia clings to dated, ineffective methods and blinds us to new methods for new seasons. Mary was so overcome with grief in the garden that she thought Jesus was the gardener, and even when she did realize who He was, Jesus had to restrain her from holding on to Him. Perhaps Mary wanted to relate to Jesus in the same way she had for the previous three years. But Jesus was about to introduce her to a new season. *'Don't cling to Me'* were His words to prepare Her for a new era of relationship with Him. The same applies to many of us; don't cling to dead relationships, dead dreams and dead methods if you want to move into next season in your life.

As I bring this chapter to a close, one thing that is imperative in applying grace for every season is the refusal to allow the traditions of men to take precedence over God's word. One of the hindrances to negotiating a change of season is the canonizing of traditions formed in previous seasons. To canonize means to 'officially declare sacred'. There is a canon of scripture, where we can claim 'divine authenticity', but we also do that with human tradition. In church we do many things based on human tradition that may not be in the canon of scripture; the days and times we meet, the way we dress; the structure of our services and style of music are largely dictated by traditions.

Sunday school for instance, is not really a biblical command, but a wonderful tradition began by Robert Raikes in 1769. (Initially, God had designed the family for the spiritual maturing of children). The times for our services on Sunday morning were designed to accommodate the mucky habits of farmers. For the evening services, in times past, they installed gas lamps for lighting, thus it began as a novelty, and was used to attract people. There are good traditions that benefit us today, but we must never elevate any traditions and give them the same authority and canonization of scripture.

A significant part of Jesus' run-ins with the Pharisees was because of the violation of traditions, particularly the 'tradition of the elders.' These were human interpretations on how to apply the law in daily life. They held their interpretations of the law equivalent to the scriptures. One example was the Sabbath. Jesus clashed with them seven times over this issue, *'Remember the Sabbath Day by keeping it holy'*, that was the law. Their interpretation of that was to decide what was work and what was not; they introduced a tradition, a practical way to apply it. The result was a ridiculous set of rules which had nothing to do with the original command. Jesus broke *their* traditions, not the law.

We also have our traditions, our own way of interpreting and applying God's word. When seeking to serve God, we must differentiate what is tradition and what is truth. The first ten years of my Church life was spent serving God in a small Pentecostal Church in Wales. On reflection, I now realize that for most of that time the traditions of man prevented me enjoying the life abundant God had made available to me. Like the Pharisees, the Sabbath was to be kept holy, no television, no work, no sport. Their tradition had nullified the finished work of Jesus and placed them back under a law the Jews had tried and failed to keep for thirteen hundred years. People like Eric Liddell were immortalized for refusing to break the Sabbath rules.

Eric Liddell refused to run in the 1924 Olympic Games on a Sunday, believing he was complying to a command from scripture to keep the Sabbath day holy. If he wanted to comply to the letter of the law, then he should not have run on the Saturday! Moses was his coach, not Jesus. So many Christians, and I was one of them, live their Christian lives in bondage because they have canonized the traditions of men. I exalted man-made tradition on an equal par with scripture and as a result, failed to negotiate the seasons of life. God requires your devotion, not your devotions. I pray that God's grace and His grace alone will help you understand; law demands your march; grace invites you to dance.

CHAPTER NINE

GRACE FOR SHAME

"Join the Navy and see the world"

The posters were plastered all over our little village in Wales. The Navy had a recruitment drive on, and this was their bait. Those words were in big black, bold letters supported by a beautiful picture of swaying palm trees and golden beaches. My brother Roland took the bait and ended up spending the next four years serving our country, mainly working on submarines. I will never forget how proud I was, when I saw him walk down our street in full navy uniform on his first leave. I would walk around our village with him as he swaggered with his big black bell-bottom trousers, his crisp white shirt and, of course, his flat-top navy cap. He was on leave for two weeks and I could detect, towards the end of his stay home, glimpses of sadness pass across his face. On the day before he was due to go back to the training camp, I heard some painful groans emanating from the back garden.

On inspection I was faced with a truly bizarre sight. My brother was throwing a large rock onto his foot repeatedly, hence the agonizing cries. When I asked him what he was doing, he replied that life in the navy *wasn't like they said on the poster. It's horrible in the navy and I'm trying to break my foot so I can stay home.*

Of course, we persuaded him that a broken foot was not the answer, and he would have to return and stick it out. He did return and eventually settled down and made a great career in communications that held him in good stead for the rest of his life. I thought about that resentment often. I thought about the disappointment experienced by my brother, believing he had been hoodwinked by deceptive advertising, and I began to realize that many Christians end up throwing a rock on their foot, wanting out of Christianity, because they were told *'Come to Jesus and enjoy a peaceful, trouble-free life'*.

So many Christians struggle with disillusionment and disappointment because what they were promised on the poster was not actually the truth. Life begins to hit their theology and discourse. The Christian life is not like the poster.

I spoke at length in a previous chapter about Paul's painful discovery regarding the suffering of grace, unless we discover that for ourselves, that usually happens when we get to that place ourselves. We will never experience the suffering of grace in our own lives. Grace is not given to make life perfect, but to perfect us when it isn't. Grace is not given so that life works out according to our plans, but to sustain us when they don't. The grace of God is not given to ensure all our relationships work out but is available to heal our broken hearts when we are betrayed. The grace of God is not experienced when the Potter places us in the shop window, but when we are marred in the Potter's hand during the process. The grace of God works best when dreams of 'best' are destroyed. Your spouse left you; your co-worker betrayed you after years of wasted mentoring; your reputation was slandered, and close friends believed the lie. But, perhaps the worst of all, is the discovery of the traitor hiding in our hearts we never realized was there. The betrayer, the liar, the deceiver, the hypocrite. The question I pose in this chapter addressing this shocking exposure is, *'What do you do, when the rooster crows for you?' What do you do when the rooster crows for you and the traitor is exposed?* I think by now you have an idea of where we're going with this and who we are referring to.

I love Peter, because he is so human, so imperfect, so fickle. So very much like us if we are really honest, and yet, to Jesus, he was perfect material through which He could display His grace, especially when helping us to understand how to deal with shame. The confession of undying loyalty by Peter to Jesus in the Upper Room was about to come back and bite him hard. Matthew 26:30-35 describes the scene.

'They sang a hymn...'.

That is very purposeful in its connection to the unfolding events in Peter's life. Many commentators believe it was Psalm 136. (Stay with me and you will see just how strategic the choice of that hymn by Jesus was to play in Peter's fight with shame.)

> *'...and went out to the Mount of Olives. On the way, Jesus told them, "Tonight all of you will desert me. For the Scriptures say, 'God will strike[a] the Shepherd, and the sheep of the flock will be scattered.' But after I have been raised from the dead, I will go ahead of you to Galilee and meet you there."*

Wow! Jesus was giving them a grace heads-up! In essence He was saying, 'in spite of your upcoming disloyalty and hypocrisy, I'm still going to lead you, love you and use you.' What a reassuring thought that is; Jesus is always ready, beyond your failure to make a way of restoration and cover your shame.

> *Peter declared, "Even if everyone else deserts you, I will never desert you."*

Peter was really offended that Jesus would question his loyalty and faithfulness, especially after receiving the status of 'Rocky'; one who is solid, dependable and loyal whatever the storm that had to be faced.

> *Jesus replied, "I tell you the truth, Peter – this very night, before the rooster crows, you will deny three times that you even know me."*

Peter should have just closed his mouth right here, but his pride in his own ability to face any challenge was incensed. Away with such a thought, and he continued to defend his corner with the following statement.

> *"No!" Peter insisted. "Even if I have to die with you, I will never deny you!"*

And all the other disciples vowed the same. And so say all of us.

The story continues in the Garden of Gethsemane, Jesus is arrested; His prophecy of mass desertion becomes a reality; and we pick up the drama in Luke 12:55-62;

> *The guards lit a fire in the middle of the courtyard and sat around it, and Peter joined them there. A servant girl noticed him in the firelight and began staring at him. Finally, she said, "This man was one of Jesus' followers!" But Peter denied it. "Woman," he said, "I don't even know him!" After a while someone else looked at him and said, "You must be one of them!" "No, man, I'm not!" Peter retorted. About an hour later someone else insisted, "This must be one of them, because he is a Galilean, too." But Peter said, "Man, I don't know what you are talking about." And immediately, while he was still speaking, the rooster crowed. At that moment the Lord turned and looked at Peter. Suddenly, the Lord's words flashed through Peter's mind: "Before the rooster crows tomorrow morning, you will deny three times that you even know me." And Peter left the courtyard, weeping bitterly.*

This is where the story now involves us. No longer can we point the finger of disgust at Peter and say, 'If I was there...' because we've ALL been there! And some of you reading these words are there now. Like Peter, you made a declaration of loyalty, then discovered the traitor lurking inside your heart. You are devastated, shocked and shamed, because in your wildest dreams you never thought that the betrayer was hiding in your heart. The rooster has arrived for you and you don't know what to do.

Captain Wainwright commanded the armed forces during the second world war defending the Philippines against a ferocious Japanese attack. General Macarthur's orders for the battle were simple, *'Never surrender'*. Wainwright fought courageously and did his utmost to hold his ground, but the Japanese outnumbered them and to save the lives of his men, he surrendered. Against his conviction, against the will of his commanding officer, he surrendered. He and his men were sent to a remote Prisoner of War camp, where the conditions were atrocious. The treatment of those captured was brutal. They were beaten, starved and humiliated, but the greatest burden Wainwright carried was his shame. Why? He surrendered against his conviction.

When I read that story, I begin to get an idea of how Peter felt when the rooster crowed. He had surrendered against his conviction. He had betrayed Jesus' loyalty with his disloyalty. His confession of faithful commitment to his Master now sounded like the harsh crashing noise of hypocrisy.

'And Peter left the courtyard, weeping bitterly'. Shame, like a decomposing dead body strapped to his back, clinging to him like a leprous skin. This wasn't just shedding tears of remorse, this was not just 'Oh well I made a mistake, God will cover it.' This was weeping bitterly. These were the tears of inconsolable grief. In shame with no hope of relief. A condemned, guilty fear awaiting judgment. These were not tears which said, *'I shouldn't have done this, I will do better next time.'* These were tears that shouted, *'There is no next time!'* Have I described where you are right now? Is there someone reading these words that has found a place to weep bitterly? Has the rooster crowed for you, and you're hiding in a dark corner where you can't even vocalize your pain? Peter surrendered against his convictions and found a place to weep and so have you. The genuine love you thought you had for Jesus in reality, because you've surrendered against your convictions morally, relationally and biblically, has been shown to be shallow and imperfect. Like Peter, you vowed to be loyal and faithful, but because you surrendered against

your convictions, your hypocrisy has been exposed. The rooster crow has exposed the traitor. It's devastating to discover your love for Him is not what you thought it was. You are heartbroken, full of shame and you don't know what to do to be restored again. Your heart cries out 'What have I got to do to get God to love me again, to prove to God I will try harder next time? What have I got to do to be accepted again, to be used again?'

The answer is so simple, so liberating; Nothing.

You just respond to what He has already done. What He said to the unfaithful disciples he says to us. *I've already gone ahead, I'm way ahead of your hypocrisy, disloyalty and resulting shame. My plans to restore you were already in place before you failed.* Our failure is not a surprise to Jesus. Restoration is not about the sacrifice we make, but the sacrifice we trust. True repentance finds its effectiveness in trusting His sacrifice, not yours. What sin have you committed which convinced you that God's done with you? Who have you betrayed that convinces you that even Jesus can't bear to look at you? Like Peter, perhaps you have misinterpreted 'the look'.

'While He was still speaking, the rooster crowed and at that moment the Lord turned and looked at Peter'

That look must have seemed to Peter, those eyes fixed on him, like lasers representing disappointment, disgust, but most of all rejection. How wrong could he have been?

During the pure torture of scourging before death by crucifixion, the soldier would stand in front of his victim to perform his horrific task. He used a piece of wood with twelve straps of leather, each strip holding a piece of iron, bone or rock. This horrible instrument of torture was viciously harnessed against the victim's body, tearing flesh, revealing bone. The Scourger stood in front of the victim to ensure death was not experienced at the torture pole, because the victim had to breathe his last on the crucifixion stake not the flogging pole. He stood in front to determine, by looking into the victim's eyes, whether life was leaving the body. If so, the flogging would stop to allow death by crucifixion to be observed. In Jesus' case, they did something strange, something different, they blindfolded Him.

They blindfolded him and said, "Prophesy to us! Who hit you that time?" Luke 22:64 (NLT).

I believe as the Scourger viciously and mercilessly tore Jesus' body apart, with a look of absolute contempt, he couldn't stand the gaze of compassion that looked back at him. Some of you have misinterpreted that look, you have been living for years believing because of what you have done, you see Him in the disgusted faces of those who called you friend. Nothing could be further from the truth.

In a short while, Peter was about to experience the truth about that look. For me, it was not a look that said, *'how could you?'* but a look that said *'I've got you. I got this; you're going to be okay'.*

Wainwright lived in that camp weighed down with shame for standing against his conviction. MacArthur finally liberated all the POW camps in Japan, but because Wainwright's camp was in such a remote place, the Commander of the camp was able to keep the truth of the liberation from him, and as a result, Wainwright continued to live in his shame for months, not knowing he was free. Satan has kept the truth of the Grace of God from many shame-filled Christians using a distortion of the truth to do so. Wainwright kept living life as a Prisoner of War, even though he was a free man.

Satan's most effective weapon against Christians who have surrendered against their convictions is not persecution, but accusation. One of the most powerful chains that can keep us captive and blind us to the truth of the Gospel of Grace that sets us free is religious tradition; principles that are taught as biblical truth but are in fact religious tradition. Both Jesus and Paul warned us of this grace-killer. "The traditions of men" spoken of in Mark 7:13 and Colossians 2:8.

When the rooster crows for you, religious tradition will force you to focus on your interpretations and force you to focus on your imperfections and decisions you make amends for by internal scrutiny expressed in some outward form of penance. (A distortion of New Covenant repentance). The focus is directed to your imperfect love for Him, your shallow passion, your hypocritical faithfulness. So, in order to compensate and show true contrition, the doorway to restoration, we go on a religious binge of emotional flagellation, self-denial, fear-drenched confession and meticulous remembrance of every detail of our sin, we then promise to never sin in this area again, begging God for another chance to prove ourselves.

Religious tradition has violated one of the most sacred institutions of the Church, the Lord's Table. Joseph Prince has wonderfully covered the amazing truth connected to the Lord's Supper, so I won't get into the finer details here. Religious tradition has so polluted what I call God's supernatural surgery, the Lord's table is for many, a place of judgment, not blessing. Nothing could be further from the truth! Our focus at the table of the Lord is not our sin, but our Saviour. The focus is not what we have to do regarding our sin, but what He has already done concerning it. *'Do this in remembrance of Me'*, not in remembrance of your sin. The emphasis as we partake from the Body and Blood is not about your love for Him; but His love for you. It's not about feasting on your imperfections, but His perfection, Psalm 27:4 says;

> *The one thing I ask of the LORD – the thing I seek most – is to live in the house of the LORD all the days of my life, delighting in the LORD's perfections and meditating in his Temple.*

The bible's focus, from Genesis to Revelation, is not about us, it's about Him. It's not about our commitment to Him but vice versa. *'This is love, not that we love God, but that Jesus loved us.'* (1 John 4:10)

The human story as lived out through the lives of His servants is one of sin, justice and disobedience. The divine story is about His love forgiveness and loyalty to us in spite of our imperfections. If you don't establish this principle in your life, you will never deal with the sense of guilt, regret and shame when the rooster crows for you.

One of the most devastating discoveries you will ever make is that however connected you think you are, your love for Him will be shown to be flawed. For many years of my Christian life, I thought it was about my depth of commitment to God that was crucial to the maintenance of my relationship with Him, but, as life, and my failure at it met my theology, in other words when the rooster crowed for me. That's when I made the greatest discovery of all. Grace alone. An understanding of those immortal words by John Newton; *'Twas grace that brought me safe thus far and grace will see me home'* became the hallmark of my Christian life. In my darker hours of disappointment and pain, through rejection, betrayal and slander and particularly failure. When my grip on Him was practically non-existent. The only reason I'm here today is because in my darkest moments, I discovered it was not about me holding on to God, but about Him holding on to me. When I wanted to give up, He didn't; when I wanted to run away, He didn't. When Peter was weeping in a dark corner, horrified at the hypocrisy of his love, he should have remembered the significance of the hymn they sang before his botch-up.

Most scholars believe the hymn that Jesus chose to sing before the mass betrayal of His disciples was Psalm 136. There are only twenty-six verses, but each verse declares the consistency of His unfailing love. *"Oh, give thanks to the Lord for He is good. His faithful love endures forever."* In other words, the New Testament equivalent declares, *"His love never fails" 1 Corinthians 13*. Twenty-six verses and twenty-six times, Jesus was declaring to His imperfect, disloyal disciples; *'I will never stop loving you, even when the rooster crows.'* I believe Jesus was embedding in Peter's heart, the truth that in order to survive the upcoming failure of desertion, disloyalty and hypocrisy, His survival was not going to depend on his love for Jesus, but on Jesus' love for him.

Our love for Him will fail, but His love for us, will never fail. Peter was about to discover what was necessary if he was to successfully finish the race on which he was about to embark. In between the courtyard denial and the breakfast of restoration, Peter would fester. Still dealing with his shame, 'perhaps', he might have thought, 'if I plunge myself into my work, it would act as an emotional pain reliever'. So, he went fishing. Many of us know how the story goes; he fished all night and caught nothing, probably reinforcing (in Peter's mind), that he was back now living under the judgment of God, which he deserved. But unknown to him, Grace stood on the shore ready to prove the exact opposite.

Sitting in his boat, head in hands, trying to block out the sound of the roosters' crow, and banish from his memory the look from what he thought, a disappointed friend. The silence was broken with the next four words that bounced on the waters of the sea, waking him up from his shame-filled coma; *'Have you caught anything?'* Peter, in no mood for sarcasm or advice to continue any conversation about catching fish frustratedly replied, *"We've fished all night and caught nothing."* Believing that was the end of the conversation. Grace was persistent. (Grace is like that, when we want to end the conversation because of our embarrassing performance, grace is persistent in keeping it open). Grace was about to show Peter its immeasurable depths and breath-taking generosity. *"Cast your net on the other side"* Out of all experience-based options; Peter, thinking, *'what have I got to lose?'* Obeyed what he thought was the most absurd advice he had even been given. He responded to the voice of grace and discovered the amazing consequence. Far above all you can ask or think.

But the lesson was not over, when you already stand open-mouthed at the undeserved generosity of grace, He goes one step further. He gives you the credit for something you never did. *'Bring Me some of the fish that you caught'*. It was painfully obvious to Peter that was an exaggeration of the facts, he had nothing to do with the bursting nets, it had nothing to do with his skill and experience as a fisherman, it had nothing to do with deserved payback, but everything to do with Grace Alone. Grace gives you something you never deserved and gives you the credit for attaining it. Stunned by what had just happened and how a realization of just who it was that was calling him to come ashore. Peter dived into the water fully clothed to find Grace ready to serve him and de-shame him. When the rooster crows, declaring your failure, your part to receiving depends on you accepting four things.

1. You are unconditionally loved. Nothing can separate you from it.

2. You are totally known. Your failure and disloyalty have not taken God by surprise. Psalm 139:16: *Your eyes saw my substance, being yet unformed. And in Your book they all were written, The days fashioned for me, When as yet there were none of them.*

Grace had shown Peter undeserved generosity, embarrassing acceptance, now he was about to experience true humility. The arrogance of an elder-brother-spirit had to be broken. The pharisee had to be killed, the self-righteous bans of blessing had to be demolished and Jesus did it masterfully and mercifully in three repeated sentences, *"Do you love Me?"*

There are three words used for love in the Greek language; *Eros*: erotic love; *Philia*: friendship love; *Agape*: unconditional love. Jesus asked Peter the first time, 'Do you *agape* Me?' In the Upper Room, Peter would have undoubtedly answered in the affirmative, but now the rooster had crowed, the arrogance had been exposed and Peter realized he had been disqualified from such a confession. So, humbly, he responded, 'You know I *philia* You.' (Lord You know I love you dearly, but I can no longer boast of agape love, my love is flawed and I'm ashamed of that). Grace probes again, 'Peter, do you *agape* Me?' For Peter, the pain is too much to bear, the open word stings as the salt of healing is poured in, because that is what this process is about. The Master Surgeon was skilfully removing the shame of an imperfect performance, the shame of missing the mark, the shame of expressed sin, in order to show Peter, the basis of all ministries for him is grounded in His faithfulness, His love and His commitment to us, not vice versa. He was helping Peter to see it is grace and grace alone that empowers us to fulfil whatever calling Jesus graces us with. The breakthrough comes with the same questions asked a third time, but this time to remove the tumour of shame forever. This time Jesus asked Peter, 'do you *philio* Me?' Do you love Me as a friend? Do you have affection for Me? The reply was yes. Finally, he could say something without any trace of arrogance or hypocrisy, and also with the assurance that Jesus knew the worst about him, but still *agaped* him. (Lord, you know everything, You know I like You, You know I love You the best way I know how.) The lesson was learned, the shame removed.

God hears us not based on our agape love for Him, because not one of us can love on that level, but love is the wonder of grace, He even makes up for that flaw and gives us the love to love Him back; *"His love has been shed abroad in our hearts by the Holy Spirit"* Wow!

3. His plan for your life will prevail. All things will work for together for your good.

4. Finally, it's His faithfulness toward you that provides your destiny. What He started, He will finish. His is the divine GPS in your life. No matter how many wrong turns you make, if you can respond to His question, 'Do you love (Philia) Me? He will never rebuke you for failures of the past, He just wants to know do you love Him now.

Has the rooster crowed for you? Have you surrendered against your convictions? All He requires is humility to trust Him and come before Him honestly and uncovered. Back on the boat after catching so many fish, when the realization hit Peter that it was Jesus on the shore it says this: *"Now when Simon Peter heard it was the Lord, He put on his outer garment, for He had removed it, and plunged into the water."* That's odd, normally you take *off* your clothes before diving into the water. As I thought about that, I realized that, spiritually, I do the same, when I've failed or sinned and I know I'm about to face the One I sinned against, Jesus, how often, in an attempt to cover my shame, do I jump in the water fully clothed? Jesus doesn't want our religiosity He wants our honesty. Adam tried it because he was aware of God's judgment and ashamed of his nakedness, but God never approached Adam saying, "What have you done?" but, *"Where are you?"*

Perhaps it's time to take your first step to restoration and just tell Him where you are. In Adam's case, God didn't want to judge him but corner him. The prodigal's father did the same. The first thing he did was to throw a robe over him, covering the consequences of disobedience, selfishness and sin.

The fig-leaf of religious tradition and rehearsed, repetitive prayers can never cover your sin, only His Blood can.

> *For if our heart condemns us, God is greater than our heart, and knows all things. 21 Beloved, if our heart does not condemn us, we have confidence toward God.* 1 John 3:20-21 (NIV)

Jesus says to all of us who struggle with the shame, surrendering against our conviction, *'Please don't come before Me covered. Don't come before Me cosmetically, wipe off the lipstick of religious tradition. The eye shadow, the lipstick and the powder of performance, penance and religious professionalism. You don't need it in My presence. Divine make up has been provided by My love. Divine covering has been provided by My blood, and divine acceptance has been provided by My grace'.*

His grace is released and accessed by simple honesty. Instead of fearing and denying all of your real or imagined shortcomings, allow God to embrace your hang ups and see God pursue you through it and in spite of it all. The prodigal son never lost his identity, even in the pigsty he just lost his way. He thought the way back was a repentance properly rehearsed. All his father was waiting for was his son to come home. A robe of love was waiting to cover his shame, a ring of restored relationship was placed on his finger to reassure him of his acceptance and the shoes of purpose were placed on his feet, that declared, 'I still have work for you to do'.

CHAPTER 10

GRACE FOR SOURNESS

The life cycle of the Canadian Salmon is an amazing phenomenon of nature. As a young fish, it enters the ocean from the river in which it was birthed, spends its entire life at sea, then when full of eggs at the end of its life, miraculously makes its way back to the very same river, swims almost up to its source to lay its eggs for the next generation, and then dies in the very place it was born. Amazing and quite moving to be honest. What makes this miracle of nature even more heart-warming is the heroism this fish displays to lay its precious cargo.

Firstly, the salmon has to battle against the flow of the river, and by the time they arrive, their faces are totally disfigured by the rushing watery onslaught. Then there's the danger from fishermen, eagles and particularly the bears. Many of us have seen the drama on television documentaries, as the brave fish hurl themselves against the gushing waters of steep waterfalls using every ounce of energy they can muster; flinging themselves in total abandon against the torrential resistance only to be caught by the hungry open mouths of bears.

While watching one such documentary, the narrator caught my attention and unlocked for me a spiritual truth that forms the basis of the revelation I'm about to share with you. He drew our attention to the fact that the bears were not really after the fish, they wanted what they were carrying, their eggs. Wow! Then I saw it, Satan is not really after you, he is after what you are carrying. Your God-birthed dreams, incubated in your hearts, when birthed, could change a generation. The Bible says, through the prophet Joel, that in the last days God would raise up a generation of dreamers and, like many millions would say, *'be it done according to Your word'*. Impregnate me with a dream and when my fulness of time has come and give birth to that dream designed to bless many.

Our hearts are like Mary's womb; it's the place where dreams are conceived, incubated and delivered. Satan is not after you, he is after your dream and his targeted attack is the place of incubation – your heart. With this revelation, Proverbs 4:23 (NLT) exploded with intense relevance.

Guard your heart above all else, for it determines the course of your life.

Many of you are fighting battles in your humanity and losing. Battles with jealousy, resentment, self-pity and bitterness. It seems these negative emotions have set up camp and refuse to move. The reason you're not winning these battles is because you're fighting emotional battles using emotional weapons. You try to dislodge negative emotions by trying to 'psyche up' positive ones. The Bible says that *'we don't fight against flesh and blood,* (In other words, the battle is a spiritual one) *but against spiritual wickedness in high places.* Ephesians 6:12 (NKJV). *The weapons of our warfare are not carnal* (emotional, psychological, human), *but mighty in God for the pulling down of strongholds'.* 2 Corinthians 10:4 (NKJV)

What I have just disclosed to you is the battle for your heart. Satan's attempt to destroy and pollute the incubator. He's after those eggs. James discusses the battlefield even clearer in James 3:15-16 (NLT);

For jealousy and selfishness are not God's kind of wisdom. Such things are earthly, unspiritual, and demonic. 16 For wherever there is jealousy and selfish ambition, there you will find disorder and evil of every kind.

This is not an emotional battle, it's a demonic one. Demons are invoked. Bitterness, jealousy, selfishness and resentment are the predatory bears after your eggs. These destructive emotions are the oxygen which demons thrive on to wreak havoc on your life. Satan tries to attack our humanity to pollute our Christianity. In Luke chapter 11:24-26, Jesus lifts the veil between the earthly dimension and the spiritual one, and in doing so exposes Satan's strategy to pollute your heart – God's incubator of dreams.

"When an evil spirit leaves a person, it goes into the desert, searching for rest. But when it finds none, it says, 'I will return to the person I came from.' So it returns and finds that its former home is all swept and in order. Then the spirit finds seven other spirits more evil than itself, and they all enter the person and live there. And so that person is worse off than before." Luke 11:24-26 (NLT)

Demons seek dry places. There are dry places that sometimes God creates, places of testing to develop our character. But the dry places described by Jesus here are ones that we create, allowing Satan to prevent our dreams being birthed. Jesus tells us that demons seek dry places, because they can cause havoc in dry places; they can kill, steal and destroy in dry places. They can destroy marriages, split churches and even cause suicide in dry places. The devil seeks dry places, places of poor irrigation. Places where there is absence of water. 1 Peter 5:8 (NLT) says,

> *Stay alert! Watch out, for your great enemy, the devil. He prowls around like a roaring lion, looking for someone to devour.*

What's he seeking? Dry places. With this reservoir of revelation to work with, the words of the apostle Paul, to the Ephesians, puts the whole thing into context and actually describes the dry places in more detail. Ephesians 4:27 (AMP),

> *And do not give the devil an opportunity [To lead you into sin by holding a grudge, or nurturing anger, or harbouring resentment, or cultivating bitterness].*

Now these are not emotions or attitudes he'd just pass through us, but ones we invite to stay. Look at the adjectives used; 'holding a grudge'. In other words, 'this is mine; I'm keeping it and I'm not letting go.' Nurturing anger. We must look closer at the vocabulary,

Nurture: 'to care for and protect something, encouraging it to grow, perpetuating its life.'

Harbouring resentment: 'to give a permanent place of rest. Allowing it to drop anchor in your heart.

Cultivating bitterness: to provide suitable soil, fertilizer and environment for a plant to grow, and to daily attend to its development.

If I were to paraphrase that verse as described in the Amplified Version, it could possibly read like this. *'To refuse to let go of a grudge, and to actually take care of and protect negative anger, helping it to develop and perpetuate its life, to give shelter, protection and hospitality to resentment, giving it a place to stay and to daily tend to bitterness like a plant, ensuring the soil of your heart is a dry place for devils to walk'* (PP)

Holding grudges, nurturing anger, harbouring resentment and cultivating bitterness produces barren wastelands where devils long to walk. That's why Paul was so passionate for us to get rid of them. Ephesians 4:31(AMP) tells us

> *Let all bitterness and wrath and anger and clamor [perpetual animosity, resentment, strife, fault-finding] and slander be put away from you, along with every kind of malice [all spitefulness, verbal abuse, malevolence].*

The Bible instructs us to resist the devil, NOT assist him! If we are going to be people who desire to incubate and give birth to God-given dreams then we have to guard, above all else, that place of incubation.

In contrast, if the devil seeks dry places to pollute, the Holy Spirit seeks watered places to create. As Satan seeks dry places, the Holy Spirit seeks wet places. He is attracted to water. He moves creatively over wet places. The Bible gives us beautiful illustrations of this in both Old and New Testaments. In Matthew 3:16 it states,

> *After his baptism, as Jesus came up out of the water, the heavens were opened, and He saw the Spirit of God descending like a dove and settling on Him.'*

The Holy Spirit seeks wet places to settle, to anoint. The story of Creation can give us a wonderful practical illustration of this truth in Genesis 1:1-2 NLT,

> *In the beginning God created the Heavens and the Earth, the earth was formless and empty, and darkness covered the deep waters. And the Spirit of God was hovering over the surface of the waters*

Wet places attract the favour and creative power of God. A place where He can create order out of confusion; beauty out of ugliness; fullness out of emptiness; light in the darkness. A place where God declares *this is My beloved Son in whom I am well pleased.*

* * * *

Bitterness, resentment, strife and anger create ugly worlds and dry hearts.
'It's time to close the airport.'

These words were spoken to me when my heart was being scorched by bitterness, anger, jealousy and resentment. I could sense demons lining up to run rampant in the dry places as I cried out to God for help. Having endured a season of 'long-suffering' as a result of slander, betrayal and incredible heartbreak; I was at the point of desperation as these hellish emotions were gradually turning my heart into a dry wasteland.

I was travelling by car to Heathrow Airport, London, fighting this turmoil in my heart. As I neared the airport, the sun was setting, and I could see the planes coming into land. The fading light highlighted the headlights on the airplanes as they descended. At one point, I could see at least five or six planes lining up in formation as they approached the runway. I thought to myself, 'that's a picture of the battle for my heart right now.

The first plane about to land is resentment, I'm going to have to spend a lot of emotional energy dealing with that, and at the same time deal with the anxiety that anger was touching down minutes later, followed by bitterness, jealousy and a host of other unwelcome incomings. In frustration, I cried out to the Lord, 'please strike down the planes!' What He replied to me that day changed my life forever and practically made sense of everything I've written in this chapter;

Why don't you close the airport?

Devils cannot land on Word-covered Runways; bitterness cannot land on grace-covered runways; anger cannot land on praise-covered runways; grudges cannot land on forgiveness-covered runways. Flood the runways! Close the airport!

His response took my breath away, and I realized I don't need to fight these emotional battles using emotional weapons. I just need to flood the runways with grace, love, praise, forgiveness and, particularly, thanksgiving. I pray these words are beginning to flood your heart with hope as perhaps you too are dealing with some destructive emotions. The only criteria for God to open up Heaven's floodgates and flood your runways is trust.

I knew I qualified that day for a deluge, I had come to the end of myself and, emotionally exhausted, I cried out with the Psalmist, *'Oh God, You are my God, early will I seek You. My soul thirsts for You, my flesh (emotional life), longs for You in a dry and thirsty land where there is no water.'* (Psalm 63:1 NKJV)

His response? Isaiah 44:3a (NKJV) *For I will pour water on him who is thirsty, And floods on the dry ground.* It's time to drown some devils! When we cry to God from a thirsty heart, it looks like a tsunami to the devil.

An often-misquoted verse from Isaiah can clear up a big misconception about the battle for our hearts. It's found in Isaiah 59:19. Before we read the verse, it's important to realize that the Old Testament scriptures, when written in their original form, were written without punctuation and after being translated into English, because of the structure of our language, punctuation was required to make sense of the sentences. I personally believe reading chapter 59 of Isaiah, within its context, the translators misplaced a comma; presenting the devil in a much bigger and more threatening way while we cower under his onslaught. Part of that verse says *when the enemy comes in like a flood, the Spirit of the Lord will rise up a standard against him.* Even with the mispronunciation it's not a disaster, for the Lord still has the upper hand, but the way it is written gives the impression the enemy is a mighty rushing flood, and we have to brace ourselves from the approaching evil tsunami, when in fact the opposite is true.

In context, it should read like this, "When the enemy comes in, [then] like a flood the Spirit of the Lord will raise up a standard against him." That changes the picture doesn't it? That's what happens when we decide to flood the runways, using our spiritual weapons to close down the airport.

I've mentioned thanksgiving, or a spirit of thankfulness, as a powerful weapon to irrigate dry hearts and flood runways. Because thanksgiving is particularly powerful to flood the runway of resentment when betrayed. When Jesus was attacked emotionally with betrayal and satan was nearby, seeking a dry place in His heart to land his plane of resentment. He had to seek elsewhere. The airport was closed to him, and the runways flooded to his evil touchdown because of the power of thanksgiving. Jesus' heart was saturated with thanksgiving. He could even take His betrayers' feet in His hands, the same feet He knew were about to walk into the enemy's camp and sell Him for thirty pieces of silver, and wash them.

The scriptures describe it this way, *In the same night He was betrayed… He gave thanks…* (1 Corinthians 11:23-24)

Satan had tested something else to land his plane, in fact, he had already landed the plane of treachery on the heart of Judas, taxied up to the gate and its evil cargo was now disembarking into every crevice of Judas' dry heart. Jesus didn't thank God for the betrayal, but the sovereignty of His Father in spite of it. On one occasion Jesus said, *'no-one can come to Me unless the Father allows it'* (John 6:65 NLV). It's time to close the airport. It's time to flood the runways. It's time to drown some devils. I don't know what has caused the heartbreak. I don't know why that tragedy happened, or those people betrayed you, but I do know this, how you respond is crucial to the fulfilling of your destiny and giving birth to that dream.

Satan is after those eggs; Satan seeks a dry place. Irrigate your heart with thanksgiving; *In everything give thanks; for this is the will of God for you in Christ Jesus for you.* 1 Thessalonians 5:18 (NKJV).

My friend, Terry Law, founded a unique singing group in the seventies. He had a vision to use the power of praise and worship to break chains and set people free. The group were named *Living Sound* and God opened the door for them to countries which previously had been closed to continental missionaries. They saw thousands come to Christ through their music and testimonies. Terry had a beautiful wife and three small children. Whilst in London on one trip, his associate woke him up in the middle of the night to inform him that his wife had been killed in a car accident. He thought he was dreaming, then, when the reality of the news sank in, he felt himself sink into a hole of grief he thought he would never get out of. On the flight home, satan had all his planes lining up to land on Terry's heart, and as Terry laid down his desires, one by one the devil landed his planes; resentment; bitterness; anger; disappointment. The airport was open, he had found a dry place.

For months Terry battled with the pain and the loss. Not only had he lost the love of his life, but the passion in his heart. Understandably, he questioned God as to why this tragedy had come to his door. After giving his life sacrificially for fulfil God's call on it, why was this happening? As the depression deepened and the enemy's planes continued to land, Terry resigned himself to the fact that he would never be able to serve God as a minister again because of the dryness in his heart. A close friend observed Terry's demeanour and language during this season and advised him to spend some time each morning simply thanking God. Terry's initial response was one of disbelief, but his friend insisted that Terry take that verse *"In all things"* (not for all things) and start to give thanks to God *in spite of* the tragedy. With absolutely no genuine desire to take his friends advice, he did it anyway. For days and weeks, he gave himself diligently to this exercise of thanksgiving, until one day, something happened; the heavens were opened, lifegiving water flooded the runways, devils were drowned. The airport was closed once and for all to demonic landings and from that time until his death in 2020, Terry terrorized the enemy camp all over the world. He eventually wrote a book resulting from that experience called *The Power of Praise and Worship*.

Do you need to close the airport? Are the runways of your heart cluttered with the enemy's fleet? Come on! It's time to flood the runways, close the airport and then lay those eggs!

CHAPTER ELEVEN

GRACE FOR SURRENDER

In Mark 8:22-25, we encounter Jesus healing a blind man through a second touch. The first time Jesus touched him, he could see a little, but explains his vision was still blurred and men were like '*trees walking*'. He could see but needed Jesus to touch him a second time to have twenty-twenty vision. Seeing, but not seeing is a common problem in the church. Christians can see that Jesus carried their sins, but still there's a problem with guilt and condemnation. Christians can see Jesus became poor that we might become rich, but still have a problem with God's generosity toward them. Could our dilemma be mirrored in the story of the blind man? We need the miracle of sight (salvation) but need a second touch for us to truly see the rest of it clearly. Over the past fifteen years, that is what has been happening to me. In fact, in certain areas relating to the wonder of the grace of God, it's been multiple touches as the Holy Spirit has been pulling back the veil, allowing heavenly light to make things much clearer. I believe a vast number of the body of Christ needs a fresh touch, so that they can see clearly the breath-taking scope of God's grace.

Peter needed a second touch. He believed the power of the gospel but had a problem seeing it working beyond the borders of the Jewish nation. He saw, but he didn't see. So, on a rooftop at three in the afternoon, Jesus touched him again and opened his eyes to the unprejudiced nature of the gospel by grace and as a result brought the gospel to the Gentiles. His law-based parameter could not embrace the immensity of the inclusive nature of the grace of God. He was about to learn through the vision on that rooftop, that grace cannot fit into the limitation of the law.

I read a story that, for me, perfectly illustrates Peter's problem: Two fishermen were fishing close to one another, when one fisherman noticed his neighbour was keeping the small fish he was catching and throwing the large fish back. When questioned about it, he replied, 'Well, the big fish won't fit into my frying pan!' So many believers do not enjoy the freedom of grace-based living, because they're trying to fit the message of grace into the legalistic 'frying pan' of law. His generosity is too big; His unconditional love is too big; His no-strings-attached forgiveness is too big. You either keep the fish and throw away the frying pan or vice-versa. The message of grace cannot fit into the small, restrictive frying pan of the law. Grace doesn't undermine the law; it simply negates it.

In the case of the woman caught in adultery, the law had to leave once it fulfilled its purpose: to bring the guilty to the feet of Grace. Once that had happened, the law left. From the 'oldest to the youngest', leaving the condemned woman at the feet of Grace alone. The law was unable to maintain credibility of position within the company of grace. Grace and law could not coexist in the same room, one had to leave, and it wasn't grace. You don't boast about your crayon sketches in the presence of Michelangelo. You don't impress NASA technicians with your paper plane, and you don't boast about your law-based performance, piety and holiness in the presence of perfection. Paul, writing to the Ephesian Church, prayed that Jesus' would touch them again. Paul prayed they would receive a second touch, that their eyes would be opened to understand what was accomplished through the finished work of Christ. (Ephesians 1:15:23) The Ephesians saw 'men as trees, walking'; they saw it intellectually but needed a second touch to enjoy it exponentially.

So many preachers are exhorting what we should do. We need more to declare what Jesus has already done. I say all that to introduce the subject we are addressing in this chapter. The Holy Spirit gave me a second touch regarding the word that has revitalized my work with God. Repentance. So many believers live a 'yo-yo' Christian life. A 'He loves me, He loves me not' relationship, all because of one of the most misrepresented doctrines in the New Testament. The doctrine of repentance. As I see it, the charismatic church has reinvented the whole concept of repentance or, as I like to term it, 'surrendering to the will of God'. For too long the church has been a place where a guilty preacher has been teaching a guilty congregation how to feel more guilty and to produce a guilty response. Repentance based on guilt will never last, we flock to the front to cry our guilty tears to release our guilty emotions and come back next week and do the same. God never uses guilt in a believers' life to motivate change.

This doctrinal pollution kept the church in chains for centuries until Martin Luther uncovered the lie. As many of us know, Martin Luther, who lived in the 16th Century, was a Catholic monk who nearly killed himself striving to please God through law-based living because of the perversion of one word, 'repentance'. While teaching at a university, studying the New Testament from the original Greek text, he realized he'd been lied to for years through the Latin translation. When translating the Greek New Testament into Latin, the Roman Catholic Church translated the word 'repentance' as 'Do penance'. In other words, favour with God when you sin is only restored when penance is observed. Do something to show how sorry you are about your sin, that could range from reciting some chant, to self-flagellation, to lengthy fasting. The focus was on behavioural change. When Martin Luther read the Greek meaning of the word repentance, it changed the course of Church history. The word for repentance in Greek is *'Metanoia'*, which simply means to change the way you think; change your mind.

Redirect the way you think; when that happens, behavioural change will be the result. The reason why law-based living (religion) thrives is because it involves two elements: an angry God, and a guilty conscience. It's the treadmill for an unhappy life! Luther lived on that treadmill for years until he received a second touch which destroyed it forever. Not only did the correct translation of repentance express the ineffectiveness of the doctrine, but also the focus. Remember, the focus of repentance in the New Testament was not predominately sin, but God. Change the way you think about God; when you realize God is not angry with you even when you sin, the revelation of His goodness will motivate you to change based on gratitude and not guilt. Paul's preaching on repentance focused more on changing the way you see God, more than turning from sin.

Testifying to Jews, and also to Greeks, repentance toward God and faith toward our Lord Jesus Christ. Acts 20:21 (NKJV)

When you change your mind about God, the result will be repentance or a turning from a sin, it's ...*the goodness of God that leads to repentance.* (Romans 2:4 NKJV).

An understanding of New Covenant repentance is the key to the effective communication of the gospel of grace and to living in the joy of it. The picture that comes to mind when we think of New Covenant believers living with an Old Covenant concept of repentance is like someone hugging a cactus, the more we hurt, the more genuine the repentance. Many believers have hugged the cactus of penance-based repentance, not knowing whether this repentance is deep enough or sorrowful enough to match their sin. Have we relegated New Covenant repentance to the emotional realm, where the genuineness of our repentance is measured by whether we've cried enough, felt ashamed enough, or don't feel guilty enough? We have equated repentance with morbid introspection and regret, coupled with a deep sense of remorse and shame. Self-reproach and condemnation expressed with a prostrate body and wet cheeks. We believe that only when God sees this in us (and only He knows when we've passed repentance criteria) will He move in kindness toward us. Many believers cower under the conditional recipe for relationship with God that is totally dependent on the depth of their repentance, rather than the depth of God's grace.

Many feel alienated from God because they can't fulfil the 'if' ingredient demanded by 2 Chronicles 7:14, *If My people, who are called by My name will humble themselves, and pray and seek My face, and turn from their wicked ways, then I will hear from heaven, and will forgive their sin and heal their land.* I am writing these words while on lockdown in Durban, South Africa, because of the Coronavirus Pandemic. I am saddened that many preachers are bludgeoning us with this verse, as though God is holding us to ransom for this virus that's killing thousands. The enemy is using this verse to dupe the church into beating herself up with guilt and morbid introspection, believing God is sitting in heaven with folded arms waiting for the repentance level to hit 'heal' and 'forgive'. He is laughing at our ignorance and self-righteousness while the virus runs rampant unrebuked.

When the disciples were hit by a storm while Jesus was asleep in the boat, they panicked and woke Him up. He rebuked the storm and then turned to them and said, 'Where's your faith?' Not, 'where's your repentance'! He didn't say, 'I'm not rebuking this storm until I see some level of repentance for your thoughts of unbelief' Not at all! The same applies to any storm that hits, instead of trying to fulfil the 'if' in 2 Chronicles 7:14, why don't we pray the prayer of those imperfect believers in Acts 4:29-30:

Now, Lord, look on their threats and grant to Your servants that with all boldness they may speak Your word, by stretching out Your hand to heal, and that signs and wonders may be done through the name of Your holy Servant Jesus.

Their focus was on New Covenant faith, not Old Covenant repentance; that demanded holiness and repentance based on judgment, not grace. We must realize that the Cross changed everything. The wonderful message of grace has deleted the 'if' based on performance and replaced it with belief based on grace. Ephesians 2:8-9 (NKJV) Tells us that Christianity is not the sacrifice we make, but the sacrifice we trust:

For by grace you have been saved through faith, and that not of yourselves; it is the gift of God, not of works, lest anyone should boast. Religion says, 'behave to be accepted, grace says 'believe that you are accepted'. Matthew 11:28-30 MSG says,

"Are you tired? Worn out? Burned out on religion? Come to me. Get away with me and you'll recover your life. I'll show you how to take a real rest. Walk with me and work with me – watch how I do it. Learn the unforced rhythms of grace. I won't lay anything heavy or ill-fitting on you. Keep company with me and you'll learn to live freely and lightly.

For years I hugged the cactus of law-based repentance to perfect personal holiness; not only did it rob me of joy, but it turned me into a judgmental pharisee. Because we have a distorted perception of vertical grace, there is a famine in the Church of horizontal grace. A beautiful picture of this can be seen in God's instruction to Moses as to the design of the Ark of the Covenant. On top of the Ark, beaten from one piece of gold was the Mercy Seat. Its dimensions, bigger than the Ark itself, beautifully illustrates to us that mercy is always bigger than law. Blood of a sacrificed animal was sprinkled on the Mercy Seat because God's focus was on the blood sacrificed animal to atone for their sin, not the behaviour of the priest. Each side of the Mercy Seat, beaten into shape out of the same piece of gold, were two Cherubim. They were to be facing each other, but not looking at each other, they were to be looking down at the mercy seat where the blood was placed. The lesson? If they looked at each other, they would just see a replica of themselves, with the same flaws and imperfections, but when they looked down, they saw each other in the reflection of the blood. We need that spirit in the church, to kill our pharisaic, judgmental attitude toward each other, and begin to see each other through the reflection of The Blood. The moment the focus of your life shifts from your badness to His goodness, the result is repentance.

The key to the power of the gospel is the declaration of forgiveness of sins and people's acceptance of it. The gospel is the power of God to those that believe not repent. Faith accesses the power of the gospel, not repentance. The only sin that God sees when He looks at the world through the cross is forgiven sin. The first time the gospel was presented to non-Jews, the Holy Spirit intercepted Peter's sermon at a key point. Acts 10:43-44 (NKJV):

> *To Him all the prophets witness that, through His name, whoever believes in Him will receive remission of sins." While Peter was still speaking these words, the Holy Spirit fell upon all those who heard the word.*

Repentance was not demanded before forgiveness was received. But it was demonstrated *after* forgiveness was believed and received. They were baptized. When Paul was asked that hell-avoiding, eternity question by the Philippian jailer, *'What must I do to be saved?'* Paul's answer determined the eternal fate of the jailer's soul. This was his answer, "*believe in the Lord Jesus and you will be saved*". When John the apostle penned the immortal, iconic words of Jesus in John 3:16 to a fallen world, God's key to eternal life and deliverance from the kingdom of darkness was made available to 'whosoever believes'. In fact, the gospel of John, arguably the most read gospel, never mentions repentance as the criteria to God's blessing, but mentions 'believe' seventy times. Listen to Paul's words again in Acts 13:38 (NKJV):

> *Therefore let it be known to you, brethren, that through this Man is preached to you the forgiveness of sins.*

The parable of the Prodigal Son is a masterpiece, painting the true colours and texture of New Covenant repentance. When the prodigal limped home from his lengthy binge of wandering, boozing and womanizing, his motives were mixed at best. Repentance for breaking his fathers' heart was not his primary concern, it was personal survival. *"How many of my fathers' paid servants have more food than they want and here I am dying of hunger? I will leave this place and go to my father..."*. Disappointed with life, he made his way home, not from a burning desire to see his father, but to just stay alive. Even his repentance seemed mechanical, rehearsed and selfish. 'I will go home and say this, this and this!' The father saw through all of it. He was not concerned about the sons motive for going home, he was just overjoyed that he came home.

The lesson here is a powerful one, we don't have to wait until our hearts are pure or our rehearsed repentance seems genuine. We don't have to be shredded with sorrow or crushed with contrition. We don't have to be perfect or even very good before our God will accept us. We don't have to wallow in shame, remorse, guilt or self-condemnation. Even if we still nurse a secret nostalgia for the far country, God falls on our necks and kisses us. Even if we come back because we couldn't make it on our own, God will welcome us. He will seek no explanation for our sudden disappearance, He's just glad we've turned up so He can bless and restore us. Stop hugging the cactus of unbiblical, emotion-based repentance and come home.

For years my image of God was reduced to a smallminded bookkeeper logging every sin and failure for future debt recovery, or like a niggling Customs Officer rummaging through my moral suitcase. My repentance seemed more like a New Year's resolution than a genuine heart that desires to receive His love. God is not withholding His love until you walk right up to His door begging to be accepted with promises of change. No! As soon as we decide to come home, irrespective of our rehearsed repentance, our Heavenly Father runs to meet us ignoring our spiritual theatrics and just overpowers us with raging love and generosity.

I often wonder why the father ran toward the prodigal. Apart from his love, could it also have been because he wanted to reach the prodigal before the elder brother got to him? The amazing thing about God's forgiveness is that not only does He forgive before we repent, He shows us incredible generosity before we perform. The fatted calf was killed, the robe, ring and shoes were given before the prodigal produced any fruit of repentance. I am a prodigal every time I search for unconditional love where it cannot be found. Why do I keep leaving home where I am beloved of the Father, to find love and fulfilment in a pig pen, hugging the cactus of penance-based repentance believing it can transport me back to that place of unconditional love? For those of you in a far country, living in a pig pen, remember how good you had it in your Father's house. Come home, the robe, ring, shoes and celebration are waiting. Stop hugging the cactus, trying to prove your repentance has earned it. Just come home.

While travelling home on a plane from Norway, I sat by a man who had broken his foot whilst skating. We struck up a conversation and I asked him what he did for a living, he modestly told me that he was the personal portrait artist for the British Royal Family. When I told him I was a preacher, he asked me if I could help him interpret a dream that he'd had fifteen years earlier. He explained that in the dream, he was kneeling before a man, and he just knew that Man was Jesus. He started to pour out his sins to Jesus only to notice that His face was completely unshocked. He went on to explain, that, as a portrait artist he was able to put facial emotions onto the canvas, that was his gift. He continued to say 'at the end of the dream I told Jesus I didn't believe in Him. It was at that point Jesus' eyes dropped in disappointment and then I woke up.' He turned to me and asked,

"Can you tell me what that dream meant?"

"You have just visually explained a truth that theologians have used millions of words to explain! I replied, do you know why Jesus was unmoved at the revelation of your sins? Because He has paid the debt for every one of them. You are already forgiven." I continued, "You know why His eyes dropped in disappointment? Because you don't believe it."

The power of God is not activated by a confession of sin, but belief in forgiveness. Again, let me quote Acts 13:38-39 (NLT) for your meditation;

"Brothers, listen! We are here to proclaim that through this man Jesus there is forgiveness for your sins. Everyone who believes in him is made right in God's sight – something the law of Moses could never do.

Five hundred years ago, God sent Martin Luther to light up the skies over Europe with the message of the gospel of the grace of God. Shepherds were watching their flocks by night under the darkened skies of judgment-based Catholicism. Just like the shepherds who watched their flocks by night on Bethlehem's hills, so shepherds all over Europe were carrying out their ministries under the bleak skies of legalism. You know those shepherds around Bethlehem? They were specifically assigned to take care of the Passover lambs to be slain once a year to cover sin, (a temporary solution) and were instructed to go to Bethlehem. They would find there the true Passover Lamb who would take away sin once for all, for everyone. A permanent solution. God sent angels into their darkened world to declare to them a Saviour had been born, not a judge. One who was born to save the world, not condemn it. Two thousand years later, God is sending angels to light up the skies of discouraged shepherds, watching the flocks by night, ministering under the darkened skies of a law-based understanding of the gospel.

I was one of those shepherds, until God sent Joseph Prince to my hillside and he lit up the skies with the revelation that no longer am I to preach grace *a lot*, but to preach grace *alone*. The catalyst for me was a correct understanding of Romans 8:1. Until then, I believed that walking in God's grace and a state of no condemnation, was dependent on whether I walked in the spirit or the flesh. My belief, based on that verse, was that God's grace and no condemnation was dependent on my behaviour. When Joseph explained to me that the latter part of Romans 8 was not the original text, but was added by the translator, a nuclear explosion took place in my spirit, and I saw it. It's not grace-*if*. It's not grace-*but*. It's not grace-*depending*. It's grace *alone*.

There is therefore now no condemnation for those who are in Christ Jesus. Romans 8:1 (NKJV)

The light of heaven shone into my heart revealing breath-taking discoveries that have changed my life forever.

The Joshua generation had crossed the Jordan which had miraculously parted in full sight of the inhabitants of Jericho. So awesome was the sight, the Bible says, that before the armies of Israel drew a sword, the city was shut up in fear because of them. God then instructed them to do something they hadn't done in forty years. Celebrate the Passover. I can imagine the soldiers guarding the walls of Jericho, gazing out at thousands of campfires, wondering what the Israel armies were preparing to do. And then, the pungent smell of roasted lamb, carried by a gentle breeze began to slowly slide its way across the plains of Jericho, up the fortified walls and into the enemy camp. I can imagine one enemy soldier saying to another, 'why are they roasting lamb?' Perhaps the other soldier, ashen faced, would say, 'I don't know what this means, but I heard that forty years ago, they did this as slaves in Egypt and the following day the whole of the Egyptian army was destroyed.' The smell of the lamb, not the size or the strength of the army, paralyzed the enemy with fear. That truth is even more relevant for the church today. It's not the smell of denominationalism, sensationalism or emotionalism that brings fear into the heart of the enemy, but the smell of roasted lamb. The finished work of grace alone. It's the smell of the lamb rising from our preaching, our praise, our compassion and our generosity. It's what Paul describes in 2 Corinthians 2:15-16, *'the aroma of Christ'*, pleasing to God, a stench to the enemy. To the enemy it was the smell of death, but to Rahab, the prostitute that helped the Israelite spies, the smell of life.

This key to God's favour on churches for growth and influence is not the smell of Christian celebrity, technology or talent, but the aroma of the Lamb. Grace alone permeating our worship, our preaching and our lifestyle. To some, it will be an offensive smell, but to many, like Rahab, it will fill their hearts with hope, and the realization that grace has come to their door. When the revelation of grace alone sends a floodlight on law-based darkness, when the smell of the Passover lamb fills our hearts with hope, when you've been to Bethlehem and discovered a Saviour; Someone who takes your breath away, sins away, pain away and fear away. Even seemingly horrid genealogies become alive with energy because of the gospel of grace.

CHAPTER TWELVE

THE GENEALOGY OF GRACE

When reading the genealogy of Jesus in Matthew chapter one, I discovered four wonderful aspects of grace, particularly from verse 1, 3, 5-6 and verse 16-17. I call it The Genealogy of Grace. Firstly, creation teaches us how to submit to grace alone; in verse 16, *and Jacob the father of Joseph the husband of Mary, of whom Jesus was born, who is called Christ.* You may wonder what this verse has to do with the fact that creation has a greater revelation, submission, respect and acceptance for its Creator than the sons of Adam. When I read those two names united together, Mary and Joseph, in my imagination I'm standing at the door of the Innkeeper who refused grace a bed. Unknown to him, he missed an opportunity to serve and honour the King of Kings as He lay hidden in Mary's womb. At His birth, He was refused a place to lay His head by this Innkeeper, a son of Adam; but had acceptance and welcome in the shelter and the food trough of a beast. I know you may think this is an unusual take. On this verse, but for me, the mention of Mary and Joseph always takes me back to this wonderful earthy scene of Christ's birth surrounded by the beasts of the field celebrating His birth, while the world turns its back on its Saviour and says, 'stay away'.

The Bible says the whole of creation groans with anticipation and impatience for His return. Stars are instructed to operate as celestial 'Satnavs.' to guide inquisitive men to a unique baby. One who made the wood for His bed and chose His parents before they were born. Faith obeyed His command to provide tax money and sustenance for those who followed Him. The fig tree withered at His rebuke for its lack of fruitfulness. Water blushed red at His bidding and changed its molecular structure allowing Him to walk on its surface. An animal that no one had ever ridden subdued its impulse to buck as the Son of Man rode on its back to redeem mankind. Trees clap their hands as the mention of His name, stones would cry out in praise at His command. Even the secular and religious world shook their fist at their blood-splashed Creator, as creation roared its displeasure through darkened skies and quaking ground. Birds respond to His instruction to feed hungry prophets, and donkeys are commanded to rebuke rebellious ones. Seas are commanded to open and close at the breath of His mouth. Even wild beasts bow down and recognize Him as King. Mark 1:12-13 In the Message Version says:

> *At once, this same Spirit pushed Jesus out into the wild. For forty wilderness days and nights he was tested by Satan. Wild animals were his companions, and angels took care of him.*

I've always thought that Jesus' testing in the wilderness was not only intense, but dangerous. The picture of being attacked by wild animals has always been in my thinking until I read this verse as it was meant to be read. In the New King James translation, it simply says *'He was with the wild beasts.'* But the actual reality was that they were His companions. The Jews dreamed of the day when enmity between man and beast would no longer exist. Hosea 2:18 explains;

> *And I will make for them a covenant on that day with the beasts of the field, the birds of the heavens, and the creeping things of the ground. And I will abolish the bow, the sword, and war from the land, and I will make you lie down in safety.*

And Isaiah 11:6-9 says;

> *In that day the wolf and the lamb will live together; the leopard will lie down with the baby goat. The calf and the yearling will be safe with the lion, and a little child will lead them all. The cow will graze near the bear. The cub and the calf will lie down together. The lion will eat hay like a cow. The baby will play safely near the hole of a cobra. Yes, a little child will put its hand in a nest of deadly snakes without harm. Nothing will hurt or destroy in all my holy mountain, for as the waters fill the sea, so the earth will be filled with people who know the LORD.*

Here, in the wilderness with Jesus, we have a fulfilment of this prophecy, as leopard, bear, lion and wild boar came to their King, to offer Him comfort, companionship and above all, recognition of who He was. Grace alone. The second revelation I received while reading the genealogy of Grace, is that Christmas is not based on fantasy, but fact. Christmas is not a birth, but a coming, an arrival. God planned for the arrival of His Son before He even created the earth.

> *And all the people who belong to this world worshiped the beast. They are the ones whose names were not written in the Book of Life that belongs to the Lamb who was slaughtered before the world was made.* Revelation 13:8

What does this genealogy tell us about the meaning of Christianity and Christmas? The opening statement declares it clearly *'This is the genealogy of Jesus the Messiah'*. The story has factual roots, not mythological. This is history, not fantasy. Matthew does not begin the story of Jesus' birth saying, 'Once upon a time'. That's the way fairy tales, myths, legends and Star Wars begin. 'Once upon a time' signals when this probably didn't happen, but it's a beautiful story that teaches us so much. No! Matthew gives his statement upfront. To declare to the world that he is grounding who Jesus is and establishing Him firmly in history. Jesus is not a metaphor. He is real. This all actually happened. His opening statement is so important because it's not advice it's a declaration. Advice is 'to counsel about what you must do', news is 'a report on what has already been done'. The gospel is not 'good advice', it's Good News. Advice urges you to make something happen. News encourages you to recognize something that has already happened and respond to it. Advice says, 'it's all up to you to act', news declares someone has already acted. Religion is advice, Gospel is news. Religion says, 'save yourself', the gospel declares 'God has come to save you'.

At first glance, the story of Christianity seems like just another legend or fairy tale. Let's face it, it has the hallmarks of fantasy. Here is a story about someone coming from another world, another dimension, who breaks into our dimension with miraculous powers. He can control creation, raise the dead, then when His enemies put Him to death, no problem! He rises from the dead and opens up a way to an eternal Kingdom where there is no more pain, heartache, ageing or death, and all you have to do is to believe in Him. Really? Many shall read the story and place it in the fantasy section in their library, along with Star Wars and Superman. But Matthew refutes all that by grounding Jesus' story firmly in history.

He doesn't start with 'Once upon a time,' but, 'this was all planned'. This amazing genealogy of grace gets even more astounding, however, when Matthew goes on to list the real-life situations involved in making the plan come to pass for God to enter our world as a human being and He harnessed the cooperation of the most unlikely people to make it happen. As we read the genealogy of Grace in Matthew 1, we cannot help but be amazed, because a genealogy in those days was a declaration that stated to all that read it, 'this is who I am'. Today if we want to recommend ourselves to others, we list our qualifications, experience and accomplishments. During Jesus' time, your résumé was your family pedigree and tribe; the people you were connected to, constituted your Curriculum Vitae.

The purpose of a genealogy résumé was to impress onlookers, especially if your family root system was of a high pedigree. Matthew wonderfully demolishes this precedent. When it came to Jesus, he unashamedly lists the good, bad and ugly ingredients of Jesus' past extended family. Jesus' genealogy, unlike other ancient genealogies, was shocking to say the least. To begin with, there are five women mentioned, all mothers of Jesus. In those days, a woman's name was never mentioned, let alone five of them. Added to the amazement was the fact that most of the women mentioned were Gentiles: Tamar, Rahab and Ruth. They were either Moabites like Ruth, or Canaanites, like Tamar and Rahab. To the Jews these nations were unclean, they weren't even allowed into the temple to worship. But it gets worse! By naming these particular women, Matthew deliberately forces the reader to recount their sordid past. Tamar tricked her father-in-law into sleeping with her, a blatant act of incest. Rahab was not just a Canaanite, but a prostitute. 'Uriah's wife' AKA Bathsheba, we all know about her escapade with David. Why not call her by her real name? Because by calling her 'Uriah's wife', we are forced to recount David's plan to have him killed so that they could be wed.

It was out of this dysfunctional family, and out of this deeply flawed history, that Jesus came. It matters not how flawed or failed you are, God can use you. It matters not how you were born, or what family you were born into, He can use you to bring good news into this lost world. It's not about good people are 'in' and bad people are 'out'. Everyone is 'in' because of the genealogy of Grace. It's amazing that at the end of David's life, a life filled with greatness and failure, intensity and sin, because of God's grace, God's final words from heaven's perspective were these in 1 Chronicles 29:28 (NLT);

He died at a ripe old age, having enjoyed long life, wealth, and honour. Then his son Solomon (Bathsheba's son) ruled in his place.

Wow! Truly Paul's declaration in 1 Corinthians 13:5 (NIV) regarding the love of God rings true, especially in this dispensation of grace. '*Love keeps no record of wrongs.*'

As we come to the end of this incredible investigation of the genealogy of Grace, we can't help but realize, it is also a declaration of God's incredible faithfulness to fulfil His promise in Matthew 1:17. All those listed above include fourteen generations from Abraham to David, fourteen from David to the Babylonian exile and fourteen from the

Babylonian exile to the Messiah. This genealogy of grace reminds us that His plan and purpose took generations to fulfil, but He kept His promise. In fact, in the four hundred years before Christ was born, no prophets were sent to the people, let alone a Messiah. It looked like God had forgotten them.

But never judge God by your calendars, He will always burst the banks of your imagination. When it looks like everything is going in reverse regarding your destiny, God, in His incredible patience, is working for your good. He's always working to surprise you by His grace. For years it seemed God was ignoring Joseph's prayers. Betrayed by his brothers, sold into slavery, falsely accused and imprisoned, forgotten and discarded. But in the end the very people who tried to destroy him, were, in fact, the very people God used to propel Joseph to the fulfilment of his childhood dreams. As he surveyed this confused, seemingly disjointed and disastrous past, as he scrutinized the genealogy of grace in his own life, he could say to his brothers, 'You meant it for evil, but God meant it for good.' Perhaps it would be a good exercise, sometimes, to stop and take a few minutes to survey the genealogy of grace in your own life; the years you lived with the words which dominate your life, but in hindsight you realized your destiny was not a patch, it was always a quilt. Some patches were scary, some sad and tragic, some successful and sweet, but God, using His thread of sovereignty, took the good patches and the bad patches and the ugly patches, sewed them together, the thread of His grace holding everything together to make all things work together for your good. Thank God for the genealogy of grace in our lives. It's the divine thread that makes sense of the secret wars.

The genealogy of grace in my life causes me to continually live my life surprised. With all my fears and insecurities, I'm surprised He still uses me. With all my bad decisions, failures and sins, I'm surprised He still works all for my good. With all my refusals to forgive and show grace when I'm hurt or betrayed, I'm surprised that He always dispenses grace and forgiveness to me. When I want to give up and turn back, I'm surprised He never gives up on me. When I'm unfaithful in my service to Him, I'm surprised He always remains faithful to me. When I'm at my weakest, emotionally, spiritually and physically, I'm surprised He chooses these times to show His greater strength. I'm surprised when my humanity screams for answers, He gives me the grace during seasons of silence. The one thing the genealogy of Jesus can teach us, is that we are where we are; we are who we are and what we do because of the genealogy of the grace of God in our lives. Grace, and grace alone.

ABOUT THE AUTHOR

From humble beginnings in South Wales, to rock singer, and then Pastor; Ray Bevan, after his encounter with Jesus, has made it his mission to reach the world with the Gospel of Grace. After Pastoring the King's Church, in the city of Newport, Wales, in the UK for twenty-five years, he frequently travels to speak at conferences and churches of all denominations and sizes across the globe, and ministers regularly in Australia, South Africa, the USA, Asia and Europe. Now a regular on the popular Christian network, *TBN* and author of several books, Pastor Ray continues to impart in his inimitable style which includes music, laughter and teaching from the Word of God.

He is committed to preaching against the legalism which has slowly seeped into the Church and advocating for the Grace of Jesus Christ. Ray continues to live in Newport, Wales, but spends most of his time up in the air on his way to the next country to share the Gospel of Grace to all who are open to hearing it.